GANGS AND SCHOOL VIOLENCE
IN THE K-12 CLASSROOMS
AND THE COMMUNITY

Leodoro Hernandez

Trafford
PUBLISHING

 www.trafford.com

North America & international
toll-free: 1 888 232 4444 (USA & Canada)
phone: 250 383 6864 ♦ fax: 250 383 6804 ♦ email: info@trafford.com

The United Kingdom & Europe
phone: +44 (0)1865 722 113 ♦ local rate: 0845 230 9601
facsimile: +44 (0)1865 722 868 ♦ email: info.uk@trafford.com

10 9 8 7 6 5

TABLE OF CONTENTS

PART I

INFORMATION TO LEARN ABOUT THE GANG CULTURE

PART II

REFERENCES TO BE USED TO BETTER DETECT GANG MEMBERSHIP

PREFACE

Gangs in the American society are not new and have been in the American scene for years and years. However, the face of gangs is changing with the advent of youth gangs and has been increasently more and more violent. These gangs are new groups and we need to understand their culture. Yes, the new gangs have created their own subculture. The Italian Mafia is an old crime system, but if we believe the movies and TV, they have rules. Yes they kill people, but only those that are chosen to die, according to their leader, but the rest of the family is left untouched and are respected. As they often say, "it's not personal, it's business." However, in the new youth gang culture, the gangs have drive-by shooting and many innocent people are killed, and they don't seem to have any rules except to kill or be killed.

School violence is another phenomenon and this book attempts to address this issue also, but only in comparing gang to school violence, because the author is not sure if school violence is a culture, except for "bullying." Bullying has always been part of the school and community environment, but now the retributions by those that have been bullied are deadly. Consequently, these cultures, and school violence, should be part of the university curriculum in every program that prepares teachers for the new realistic cultural world.

Can gangs be eliminated? It is very doubtful especially with most governmental resources going to the war on terrorism and Iraq there are very few resources left to fight crime and gangs. However, Gangs can be reduced if we begin attacking the problem in the K-12 schoolrooms. This will never eliminate gangs completely, but the problem can be reduced if we begin working with students at a very young age, or at the 3rd. and 4th. grades and if all the citizens and agencies begin working together. As it is now, the police, schools, and other agencies are involved in fighting the gang problem, but there is very little coordination, or collaboration between all these entities. The time has come for a total community effort to be organized and be collaborative to address this issue.

The new gangs, as well as the old ones are in the business of making money by

distributing, or the sale of drugs. Even some of these drugs are new. Marihuana, heroin and cocaine have been in the communities for many years, but now there are cheaper and more dangerous drugs. These drugs are:
"Methamphetamine" that are produced as pills. Ecstasy pills cost ten cents to produce one pill and sell for up to fifty dollars on the street. Is it any wonder that we have so many drugs in society? What is more dangerous is that these new drugs are consumed by a younger population and often beginning in grade school. Methamphetamine is also highly addictive, Ecstasy is cheap to manufacture, but very expensive to purchase and consuming the pill one time can kill the user. Gangs provide a needed service to the users of drugs and this is another reason the gangs may never be eliminated. The war on drugs has been ineffective because it has targeted the supply side of the drugs and not the demand side, as it should be. This is the basic idea of "supply and demand." The war on drugs ought to attack the demand side of this war and if there is no, or small demand, the supply is sure to reduce and this will help reduce gang membership.

The goal of this book is to expose educators, parents, law enforcement, and the community at large about the culture of gangs and school violence, and hopefully save one child's life each day. This can be done and we should begin now because by tomorrow many children's lives will be lost.

In this book the author also provides a new educational paradigm for teachers, ideas and methods that will place the focus on the students and not the subject matter. The author also attempts to show how all subjects are interrelated and that subjects taught should include all other subjects instead of subjects taught in isolation. For more than a century educators have been concerned with SURFACE KNOWLEDGE instead of MEANINGFUL KNOWLEDGE. We may not have considered the difference, but without thinking we have been involved in teaching surface knowledge. What is meant by this? The overwhelming need of learners is learning for knowledge and there are two basis of knowledge. One is called Surface Knowledge and it involves memorization of facts and procedures. Yes some memorization is important, but surface knowledge is anything a robot can do. It refers to programming and to memorization of the "mechanics" of any subject. Tragically, surface knowledge isn't even taught today because the teachers are forced to "teach to the test" that all students are required to pass in the name of "accountability." If the curriculum is not changed so the students can achieve "meaningful Knowledge," gangs will flourish

Another purpose of this book is to educate, or inform the communities that include educators and parents. Without these two groups of people in the involvement many efforts to combat gang membership will be wasted. Much too often, children are being killed by other children and the schools are no longer immune from gang and other types of school violence. The time for action to reduce school and gang violence is NOW!

CHAPTER 1

EMERGENCE OF THE GANG CULTURE
IN K-12 SCHOOLS

The gang crisis is now at a critical point in the American society, but in too many communities and schools we are in denial that gangs are in the classroom. However, they exist in every state, every city, every small town and unincorporated towns, especially in the San Joaquin Valley of central California and the United States. Why are we at a critical point? In our current society we have children killing children and many of these young children could be saved if the community worked together, and the schools must be included, especially the teachers. At this time many teachers feel that they are teaching in the front lines, and society is not supporting them, as it should. The teachers are under paid, over worked, and much too often they spend their own money to serve the needs of their children.

Why society must support the teachers will be clear because gangs in the classroom is one focus of this book. The author is a Professor Emeritus, and before retirement he taught at a university in the School of Education preparing the future teachers for California classrooms. As such, he has learned, from various studies that we should be teaching about the gang culture in teacher education classes because it is a culture and if teachers devoted more time to educate the "wanna bee" or students in K-5 classrooms, perhaps gang membership could be decreased, then the teachers/schools could prevent gang membership and violence. It must be remembered that studies have shown that gang members do respect education and want it for themselves and others. But above all most gang members are far from being dumb or stupid.

Unfortunately, teachers are been placed in classrooms unprepared to address the gang problem that exists in many classrooms. It is like sending our soldiers into the battlefield before they learn how to fire a rifle. Teachers are on the front line of the battle against gangs and drugs. Yet, they are not being prepared by the universities to teach in schools that exist in the real world and instead they are being prepared for classrooms that no longer exist.

Consequently, K12 schools have become breeding grounds for gang recruitment and membership. In the past, society didn't have to worry about gangs in the schools, but this is the reality of today's schools.

The author has seen 3rd and 4th graders flashing gang signs or signals that the teachers don't detect, nor understand. Students think that being a gang member is glamorous, exciting and an easy way to make money. However, it is not and students should be taught the realities of being a gang member. Because being a gang member they will not be able to sleep because they don't know when they will die and on rare occasions a brother has to kill his own brother if the gang leader says it needs to be done. The students in elementary grades are wannabe gang members and are not yet hard-core. However, by the time they are in high school many of them have become hard- core. But even there, there is still a time to save students if teachers learn what to do to address this issue. It is precisely the purpose for writing this book. Is it the author's purpose to eliminate gangs in schools? That would be an impossible task until the total community works together on the same task. However, our goal, as educators will be to exert our efforts one day at a time and save one student's life at a time.

The universities teach method classes in Math, Science, Social Studies, and Reading. These are courses that will prepare the teachers to teach the children. However, some universities are not teaching the teachers about the children they will be teaching in the real world. Hence, the author advocates that the gang Culture ought to be part of the classes that teach cultural diversity in colleges. Knowing about different cultures is crucial for today's classrooms, but many colleges do not teach about the gang culture.

In this book, the author has taken information from many sources and has laid the information down in a way that educators, parents and others can understand the gang culture. This information has come from sources, published and unpublished articles, workshop handouts, and from the internet. The author has tried to bring all the varied information and put it in a book form, and hopefully he has accomplished the task of making the information understandable.

One of the adult's problems is that adults seldom view culture from the youth's point of view, and they should because the youth's view of the world is much different. Therefore, as adults we ought to formulate youthful mindsets that relate to youth. Why? Because adults often forget that they didn't always act, as the adults wanted them to act when they were young. They now think that they are grown and no longer behave like youngsters and it is not recommended that they do that. But they should not forget that they were once young themselves!

Therefore, we must think young if we are to understand the youth of today, or else we will do the wrong things and unfortunately, we often do the wrong things in society and our schools. The following are examples of what is meant by this.

Too often teachers and other adults of the community tell the students, "Why don't you just quit being a gang member?"/If the youth did quit they could be killed, or if they are not killed, gang members could assault the youngsters every time they are out in the open until they give up and become gang members./

In another example, the author attended a meeting that related to gang graffiti on the schools outside walls. At one point, the police officer assigned to the school said, "I know that some of you are gang members or know one. If you do raise your hand and then I'll see you in my office." One young girl raised her hand and the author thought to himself, "that youngster could be assaulted tonight if gang members learn that she was turning them in." Or as gang members would say, "snitches get stitches or end up in ditches."

Both of these examples help illustrate what we should not do in the schools because we don't think like the youngsters. We are reminded that towards his end, Picasso began painting like a child and when asked why. He said, "It took me a life time to learn how to paint like a child because that is true art!"

We don't have a lifetime to think like the young and the author's advice is that if we want to reach the kids/we must view things through their eyes and points of view. It is difficult to do sometimes. However, you must remember your own childhood to be effective.

As adults, do we like Rap music? If we don't, do you think the kids will quit listening to it when told how bad it is? Probably not, however, they may cease to listen to RAP if one day the teacher or parent says, "Wow that is some great music". Will the youth continue to listen to it? Probably not because if adults like the music then it must not be very good! None of us were saints when young and we did defy our parents one way or another because it was a challenge. The youth of today also like challenges and may defy parents and teachers. Consequently, adults ought keep in mind the following Hebrew proverb:

"DO NOT CONFINE THE STUDENTS (OR YOUR CHILDREN) TO YOUR OWN LEARNING AND EXPERIENCES FOR THEY WERE BORN IN ANOTHER TIME".

Going back to the basics

Recently gang graffiti and drive by shootings have decreased in Los Angeles and the police took all the credit for the decrease and shouted their effectiveness and the increase of new police officers paid for by the government.

What was not mentioned or known was that the decrease, in crime, was due the "gang leadership" in prison who spread the word on "the streets." They said that graffiti and drive-bys would no longer be tolerated because graffiti established territories and the leaders said that they wanted to sell drugs wherever they wanted and territories interfered with their lucrative drug money. Drive-bys were also banned because the gang members were shooting their own soldiers (drug sellers) and again they were losing drug money and it took time to recruit and train new drug dealers. They also said that if a member had to be eliminated, they had to do it in a manner that would not harm those around the victim. The gang leadership on the streets were told, by the gang leaders in prison, that if other members did not comply to get rid of them. Therefore, the credit for the decrease in graffiti and drive-bys should have been given to the imprisoned gang leadership in prison rather than the police.

Many sources in the past few years, have shown that illegal drugs are a $10 billion per year industry, and located in every city and small town in the United States. Selling drugs is like running a mom and pop store without mom and pop. For teenagers this can be a $200 a day business and the merchandise is small enough to fit inside cargo pockets of baggy pants, or loose sports jackets because boys and some girls store, cocaine, Meth, and Pain killer tablets to sell. Students in school playgrounds can smoke marihuana, or cocaine out of modified aluminum soft-drink cans.

Consequently, we can see that selling drugs for large sums of money that gang members can not afford to be "dumb", as we may tend to believe, because losing money when selling drugs could be a death sentence. Because they are not dumb, teachers, can channel their intelligence in positive ways and make them contributors to society. Teachers will have to address these issues, and find the means that can compete with the drug income that "youngsters" can earn. Moreover, many studies have shown that the key to deter gang membership is a solid and unbiased academic education and that means that educators can compete with the reality of life to help children become productive citizens and above all save lives.

Adult's actions and the future of schools

Adults must first take responsibility for their own actions and it is difficult because as contemporary people we often demand happiness 24 hours a day. Just look around, at liquor bars, restaurants, and hotels advertising "HAPPY HOUR". As a society we seem to want everything quickly and easily, and students know this. Perhaps we have been given too much too soon because there are approximately 45 million kids under age who do not see alcohol or drugs as dangerous and who are trying them at earlier ages than ever before. If the percentage of kids trying drugs stays the same, we will have 200,000 more 8th graders using drugs and drinking alcohol each year, and even younger children will be involved with drugs and alcohol either by using, or selling them. Is this not a crisis? Yes even alcohol is a problem in schools because it is easy to sell to other students. Some students store alcohol in small lemon or lime plastic containers and sell it by the squirt. The author believes that it is indeed a crisis. This also means that educators may be involved in the "drug war" while trying to teach.

The key to reversing today's "feel good" mentality is an educational program, starting at the earliest stages of intellectual development/ Where children need to be exposed to the idea that a life of sexual restraint and sobriety is indeed the preferred life style. In fact, sobriety and staying drug free could be "a high" onto its self. The question is, "do we begin addressing the gang issue now, or do we wait until more of the youth die from drug overdose, or violence?

Being proactive

Teachers are the heroes that serve as role models that the children need, and as teachers they must teach, but they will also become lifesavers for the children because they can curb youth violence and death. As educators, their mission must be to create a world in which young people will have a future and continue to build their own self-esteem. Teachers ought to care enough to not let students drop out of school and fail because if they fail then the school's failure is a precursor to the youth's gang involvement in violence and crime. It must be understood that teachers do care about their children, but now their charge has become something that they are ill prepared to address. As a society we also need to recognize that families are changing and often require special support systems in the schools, the community, and neighborhoods and society.

All must collaborate in the education of the children and to help fight gang membership and drugs in the schools. In all their efforts they must include the parents because they are the children's first teachers.

This chapter is an introduction about why teaching about gang and school violence can help the education community, law enforcement, and parents on how to reduce gang and violence activities in the schools and the total community. The following chapters address the gang culture, how teachers can help curb gangs and violence, how parents can detect gang membership of their children and how to possibly prevent all of this, and above all they can learn how to help prevent these type activities in the community, but especially in the classrooms. The book also contains chapters on gang attire, the meaning when wearing sport baseball caps they wear, a short introduction to RAP and Latino music and its influence on gangs. It also includes how to read tattoos and graffiti. Hopefully, the book will provide everyone an overview of gang and violence, but more importantly, how to help prevent these activities or behaviors.

Society should remember that gangs have their own set of reversed values, and flaunt the difference. Some use satanic symbolism and many others use and sell drugs, if they are hard-core gang members, using drugs may be discouraged. Yet, all that is required of educators is the fair treatment of all students with dignity, and by not using double standards when assigning grades and tasks. All that is required of the teacher is to teach!

Please keep in mind that the gang situation changes rapidly, if not daily.

Consequently, what is written in this book can serve as a guide, but don't expect that what is written here is the total answer. For example, gang affiliation is rapidly changing and the gangs of today are not the same as yesterday. The original affiliations and names, or of the past were the differences between rural and urban gangs. However, today, in 2005, they are mixed and one can find urban gang names used in rural areas and rural gang names in the urban areas. In other words the young gang members may not, do not know, or care about how gangs were formed in the past.

CHAPTER 2

THE GANG CULTURE

The origin of gangs is not new, but our knowledge and acknowledgement about them may be new. Consequently, the author includes this chapter in the book. Gangs began as Social clubs and Gang codes were developed. The Blacks started the gangs called the "Crips" and "Bloods" that are based on the Latino or Mexican gangs in Los Angeles California

Now there is a Re-emergence of traditional Latino gangs. Factors that need scrutiny are: "The presence of gang members in the family that can influence the younger siblings." In the schools we ought to look at school achievement and poor relationships between teachers and the diminished self-esteem of the deviant youth. The reasons for youngsters to join gangs are many and they will be addressed in other chapters. However, there are many reasons why youngsters are joining gangs.

In viewing gangs we find that: hard-core members are the most respected and they number 6%-10% of the membership. Associate members number about 50%-60% of the membership. The peripheral members or Wannabes are 30%-40% of the membership and they could be students from the fourth to the twelfth grade.

Their dress and clothing also varies, but the most obvious are NFL jackets that can mean, "Nuestra Familia Loca (our crazy family)" and this refers to the relationship of the gang family) and they are now wearing New York Yankees (NY) baseball caps that can mean "Norteño Youth." However, the clothing varies as gang members become aware that law enforcement and society learns of their dress. Group delinquency is a social activity providing those who are excluded from formal school rewards, such as high grades and college-oriented classes, with alternative sources of lower status. It is the lower status that the teachers can address in the classroom.

The underlying assumption is that many low-income and minority students are so disadvantaged in school, the family, and other non-school socialization that they cannot meet the expectation of the academic curriculum. As a consequence, their school status is low, threatening their sense of self, and generating feelings of frustration and failure. Another major problem within the classroom and school is that, within the Asian and Latin non-English speaking groups, the children tend to adapt rapidly into the American way of life and they begin losing respect for their parents and the culture of the "old country." These youth begin to lose their native language and culture, but can still communicate with the parents and quickly learn to manipulate them. Especially when the parents use the youth as their translators. By the way Educators also tend to use the children as translators without realizing that the youth are limited in the native language, and that they use this process to manipulate the parents much easier.

Studies have shown that most of these gang members view education as important, and some wanted to finish high school, and found school grades rewarding. But compared to their classmates, they experienced little academic success, had little confidence in their own academic ability, and more importantly, they perceived school racial ethnic relations and grading practices to be unfair.

Because of their relative inability to gain rewards that schools offer and their beliefs about academic discrimination, gang members invested little of themselves in the school social system.

Instead they found self-glorification in the gang, which yields high levels of satisfaction and provides them with feelings of belonging and a source of high social status and the gang becomes their family

The main reasons given by gang members to the question of why youngsters join gangs support this interpretation. The factors mentioned most frequently were:
- To be with friends (84%),
- For excitement (76%),
- To feel safe (70%),
- Dysfunctional parents at home and they view the classroom as also being dysfunctional,
- The need to belong to a family, even if it is other gang members,
- To protect their neighborhood (64%),
- One-third of the gang members in various studies reported that their parents did not know they were in a gang.

An article written, "No safe place" by a former State Senator Tom Hayden (Date Unknown) states:

Influence for gang membership by youth is, usually when a new person is convinced to join a gang for protection, or to join a family. Joining a family is something that kids need if they come from a dysfunctional family and if the classroom is also viewed as a dysfunctional place because kids don't feel safe or valued. People close their eyes and don't see the violence around them. If we feel safe we go into denial or believe that gang violence exists far away. However, gangs exist in, "the burbs."

The super predator theory is popular; it attributes violence to the human genes, for which there is no cure, except for the superior violence of the state. To locate gang violence in underlying social factors has been discredited by both the Republicans and Democrats. But neither stern punishment nor exhortations to Personal responsibility has prevented the violence. A better way to look at violence is through the mirror, as underclass mimicry of institutional violence, including state, corporate and entertainment violence. Nation-states, including our own, frequently inflict savage punishment to project power and preserve reputation. Not to do so is thought to invite aggression. We engage in arms races while gangs assemble weapons to control the drug underground. We fight over flags. The gangs fight over colors. Consequently, there is certain logic to the madness that gang member's display.

The mass media and politicians, since 1996, sounded the alarm about the rise in gangs and the New York Times and the Los Angeles Times who published graphic photos of tattooed gang members accompanied by vivid stories of their incorrigible violence. Governor Pete Wilson and Mayor Richard Riordan called for $18 million in state support for the war against gangs. State laws were passed making it a crime to "associate" with gangs, as defined by tattoos, hand signs, the word of paid informants, or undercover police. The anti-gang police units operated with secret budgets, and no civilian control.

The RAMPART DIVISION scandal shows that the police often planted evidence, framed people, administered beatings and even shot suspected gang members without cause. The police "worked up felonies" by issuing tickets for jay walking, loitering, riding a bicycle through a stop sign and other petty citations that were punishable by fines the families could not afford. From there it was a simple process of arresting them for outstanding citations and warrants, and then sending them to jail...

The Rampart scandal cannot be understood as simply another case of police brutality against innocent citizens, or even an example of racism in uniform. It is more. It is a case study in what happens when any means are justified in a shadowy war against society's scapegoats. We are exposed to violence very day on TV, violence in our towns, and neighborhoods. Violence is everywhere, but relating violence only to gangs is shortsighted because the politics of law and order diverts billions from educational programs that will prevent gang violence more than the police ever will. Today the alleged abuses read like a "how-to" for disregarding laws that limit power and authority by planting evidence, lying under oath, and beating, shooting, or framing innocent people. Is it any wonder that the gang members feel that the police are no better than they are?

Recently, the US Department of Health and Human Services estimated that there are 11.7 million drug abusers in this country, and this is not an inner-city phenomenon. The marches of substance abuse into our suburban (the Burbs) communities are well documented, and the nation's war on drugs has failed miserably, and we have yet to come up with any concerted strategy to address substance abuse. Consequently, we must become teachers that children will look up to. Children need heroes now more than ever because the children in poverty of this nation live with many monsters every day.

On December 7, 2002, an article appeared in the Merced Sun Star (page B4) titled, (gang violence) "Top L.A. Officials vow crackdown." The article also stated that 300 people have been killed and there are at least 200 gangs with 100,000 members in L.A. as of December 2002 and the gang crises remains critical because as L.A. gangs go so do other cities and states. Intervention is crucial now and not sometime in the future.

WHAT IS A GANG?

There is not an accepted definition for "Gangs." A true definition would include any organized group, such as the Boy Scouts. Therefore, we can simply say that there are gangs that conduct "positive" activities and there are other gangs that conduct "negative" activities. It is the group that is into negative things that the author writes about. In this case state and local jurisdictions tend to develop their own definitions. In this chapter, these jurisdictions search for:

1. Formal organization structure, but not a syndicate.
2. Identifiable leadership.
3. Identified with a territory.
4. Recurrent interaction.
5. Engaging in serious or violent behavior.

CHARACTERISTICS OF THE GANG CULTURE AND VIEWING GANGS AS CRIMANAL BUSINESS CORPORATIONS

Gangs have been with us since the beginning of organized society. The book of proverbs contains descriptions of elders being victimized by the youth. Gang proliferation and growth are associated with:

1. A breakdown of the family, and increased urbanization,
2. The advent of crack cocaine, tax limitations that cause measures that eliminate youth programs,
3. The reduction of meaningful jobs for the youth
4. Young adults that experience racial discrimination.

All these factors lead to alienation that leads to conflict and gang membership. Gang violence is a community problem that requires a multi-agency, and community based solutions. It is not exclusively a family, police or school problem.

More importantly, studies have shown that incarceration and suppression strategies alone will not solve the American gang problem; hence, community organizations, outreach programs and vocational training programs are required to effectively treat and prevent gang problems. The federal drug czar recently stated that prevention would be the future focus of the war on drugs because as long as there are users there will be drugs. This is a simple case of "supply and demand" that big business thrives in and let us be clear, drugs in the United States is big business. So long as drugs are big business there will be gangs involved in this effort and big money is much of their motive. Until selling drugs is no longer profitable gangs and violence will be part of the society. Society's task is that if we prevent people from consuming drugs decreasing the demand then the supply effort will be proportionately decreased.

As can be seen, gang activities have become "big business" and should be viewed as business. In the December 13, 2004 U. S News and World Report reported, FBI Director, Robert Mueller, in presenting his view of gangs, stated, (we must), "reclassify gangs from violent criminal offenders" to "criminal organizations and enterprises." Placing them on par with traditional crime families" -Page 22-. This reclassification tells us that gangs are no longer just a barrio, or ghetto problem, it is now a national syndicate or business. An enterprise and we ought to consider them as such by local communities.

The FBI is now targeting one major gang called "Mara Salva-trucha," or MS-13 that is spreading like a virus up and down both coasts." This gang is normally composed of Central Americans, who, when caught, are deported to their home country and then they spread their violence into Central America and Mexico communities and prisons. This gang was created, by Central Americans in Los Angeles California, to protect themselves from the Mexican American gangs.

Much of the gang activity is driven by the control of gang members, neighborhoods, turf and manipulation of other's fears. Gangs capitalize on the natural fears of gangs by community members. Remember that in Los Angeles the prison leaders have told the street gang leaders that there would be no more graffiti to denote turf because they do not want to be limited by turfs. These leaders want to sell drugs wherever they want. The word was out that anyone caught tagging or using graffiti to establish turfs should be eliminated. In Los Angeles today there is less graffiti than there is in many small towns and cities. Drive-bys shootings were also not allowed because they were killing too many of their trained drug dealers.

In the past decade, more youth have become gang members and more youth have been murdered, for instance, approximately 11,000 youngsters have been killed and 5, 000 have been seriously injured. Gangs tend to be cohesive and communicate through markings, graffiti, dress, language, (verbal and non-verbal), tattoos, hand signs, behavioral codes/rules, and so forth. Of the largest U. S. cities 83% report having a gang crisis. Males outnumber female gang members by about 20 to 1.

However, female gangs are a fast and growing problem. Unlike adult crime, most juvenile delinquency is committed in groups and juvenile crime has out paced adult crime in the last ten years. How many gangs are there in America? No one really knows because there are no rules on how a gang is started in the neighborhoods, or no hierarchy to follow, or any one else to confer with. Gangs begin anytime and anywhere and statistics are difficult to maintain. However, the last estimate was 1991, and that year the estimate was 4884 gangs with almost 300,000 members. In California alone it is estimated that there are almost 250,000 gang members today and it is growing rather than decreasing.

By the current year of 2004, gangs have spread to middle-class America. Gang members are no longer confined to the large urban inner cities and can be found in every city, large and small, and even in small towns with populations as low a 1000. An outline of the history of modern gangs in USA follows:

1. The first signs of Latino and Black gangs	1920s
2. W. W. II the Pachucos/Zoot suits; the Long Beach and Los Angeles riots, and heavy migration of Blacks and Puerto Ricans heading West and North in search of jobs.	1943
3. 1st. Neo Nazi movement in the US	1958
4. Prison gangs begin to form	1960
5. Black militant movement begins	1965
6. Immigration of Southeast Asians	1975
7. Crack cocaine appears on the "street-markets"	1981
8. There were between 400,000 and 1,000,000 gang members	1998

SUMMARY OF VARIOUS GANGS IN THE NATION

LATINO GANGS

The Mexican Mafia whose signs are the number 13, three fingers or 3 dots on tattoos, capital letter B with white out in the appropriate places, or the Roman numeral XIII. The number three or symbols that refer to the number 13, which is the thirteenth letter of the alphabet or the letter M. They are known as Sureños (southern). It started as an urban gang in prison. The other gang is La Familia, known as the Norteños (northern). This gang began with rural gang members. Because the urban and rural cultures are distinct the norteños formed their own gang. Their sign is the number 14, XIV or 4 dots on tattoos. Needless to say the number 14 is the fourteenth letter of the alphabet, which is the letter N.

Today this distinction is very cloudy probably because the gang members don't know the cultural history of gang development in the prisons. There are now urban, sureños and rural norteños in rural areas such as the towns of the San Joaquin Valley of California there are also members who call themselves sureños. The urban and rural gang membership has divorced themselves from the traditional definitions of gang memberships. More importantly, they are sworn enemies and they kill each other sometimes on a weekly basis.

DETAILS OF LATINO GANGS

"La eme" the 13-letter m in Spanish was probably the first contemporary (1960s to the present) Latino gangs that began in prison. Historically this is where the leadership formed and the gang that called itself la "eme." Some of the leaders of the eme are still in prison but until recently they controlled the gang members outside of prison, or gangs in the streets. But as was mentioned above, these gang memberships have become very cloudy as gang membership increases. Many gang members are not controlled from the prison leadership and are now in many rural communities. The same can be said about the "familia gang members.

In the beginning the "eme," was started by the East LA prisoners and other large metropolitan areas in southern California. When the prisoners that came from urban areas they did not speak much Spanish and when they did speak Spanish it was mostly "slang."

However, in the year 2004 mafia, or "eme" members called sureños are found in small towns/cities of California. This is where the prison leadership becomes cloudy because, as was stated above, often there are no rules to follow on the streets, as there are in the Italian mafia. Therefore, control of the street gangs is a cloudy issue. Consequently, there are sureños and norteños in the rural areas of

California and the rest of America. The sureños and norteños no longer abide, or adhere to the historical background of gangs.

In the beginning the Sureños, formed alliances with the Aryan Brotherhood (to be discussed later). They were very sophisticated and controlled the narcotics going into the prisons and sell them out in the streets. The gangs outside would take the narcotics into the prisons and the insiders would then control them for other prisoners that would use them. To accomplish this, they had to be sophisticated and have alliances inside and outside the prison.

The rural prisoners formed the gang called Norteños, or "La Familia. This gang was also formed in prison because they had a different culture than did the urban prisoners, and they adopted the name familia (family) in keeping with their culture. The rural prisoners, originally came from the small rural towns and they adhered to the rural Mexican culture and usually spoke Spanish and adhered to a rural culture.

However, in this 21st. century gang territories and alliances are not historical. In prison, the familia aligned with the Black Guerrilla Family (BGF). Because they are from the rural areas of California, many are farm workers or come from rural or farm worker families. The familia is found in mostly rural towns and areas of the San Joaquin valley in California. The distinction between them is that the Mafia started first in prison by the Los Angeles and other urban prisoners and the rural prisoners had a different culture, goals, and values and they formed the Familia gangs in order to survive in prison.

However, now both gangs exist in the rural towns of northern California. As recently as March 26, 2002 there was a shooting of a gang member for wearing the wrong color in Livingston, Merced County, California, The victim was a Sureño.

Consequently, the general information presented in this book changes rapidly, but the information will give the readers some ideas related to the gangs and their geographical areas. Each gang has it's own method of exterior identification and this can present clues to the readers about identifying gang members.

The Sureños markings can also appear as tattoos, symbols placed in their lockers, lunch containers, used on graffiti, or any other place that is obvious to other members around them and indicates their territory. One sign that is obvious is how they button the top of their over sized shirts, three buttons open or closed is this gangs sign. The Sureños color is blue and Norteños is "red."

It must be remembered that the Norteño's numbers are 4, 14, or IXV which is the fourteenth letter of the alphabet and like the Sureños their marking appear as tattoos, placed in their lockers, lunch containers, used on graffiti, or any other place that is obvious to other members around them and indicates their territory. One sign that is obvious, is how they button the top of their over sized shirts, four buttons open or closed is this gangs sign.

As was mentioned above there is now a gang named, "Mara Salva-trucha," or MS-13 that has already spread like a virus up and down both coasts. Including the

Carolinas, Florida and the other Northeastern states and into Central Americans and then they spread their violence into Central American communities and prisons. This gang was created, by Central Americans in Los Angeles California, to protect themselves from the Mexican American gangs.

LATINO GANG BEHAVIORS:

The Latino gang members often identify themselves, or are identified, by others, as "vato locos" (crazy dudes) and may be involved in drive-by and walk-by shootings. They have their own set of reversed values, and flaunt the difference. They use the Middle finger (giving the finger) to school and society. Some use satanic symbolism, but may not be members of a cult, unless some readers consider a gang a cult. Most members use and sell drugs if they are hard-core gang members, they may use other drugs, but they don't use the drugs that they sell, or as gang members say, "Don't get high on your own supply."

The kids that write graffiti on walls and bridges are known as taggers. They are into graffiti and are proud of their work, but are seldom violent. Their purpose for tagging, or writing graffiti is to "brag" and often leave their name used for tagging that is known as the tagger's "moniker." They also feel adult imposed rules and laws as a challenge to break the rules and laws by displaying their work in many public places and freeway bridges that to adults seem very dangerous. This activity is dangerous, but that is another of the youth's challenges.

THE GROWING GIRL'S ROLE IN GANGS

Teen-age girls, have historically been a sideshow for the male-dominated Gangs. But just as women have taken on more assertive roles in society, girls who belong to gangs are gradually shedding their subservient image and earning the same respect, attention, and are feared as much as their male counter parts. Equal rights have hit the gang culture. Girls, especially those in middle schools are drawn to the secretive world of colors, hand signals, and violence.

According to the Modesto Bee Newspaper In Modesto California:

Girls not yet in gangs say, "older guys" at parties drive by in their cars and do their Norteño whistle, "said a 12 year old girl" with braids tucked behind a black bandanna. They tell me that I am pretty, and that is about all it takes for many of us young girls to get involved with gang members. These girls are eager to please, and they want to fit in and sex is the number one way for a girl to fit into a gang. Recently there has been a lot of girl "wannabe's" gang members in California, and most of the girls in juvenile hall are in some way helping out gang members. This is fading as the girls form their own gangs. Overall rates of juvenile crime are declining, but girls now make up a larger proportion of those arrested, jailed or on probation. Girls younger than 18 make up 27 percent of all US juvenile arrests in 1999, and are up from 22 percent in 1986. An average of 15 to 20 girls are incarcerated at any given time in rural Stanislaus (California) County Juvenile Hall, and about 75 percent of them are there because of gang affiliation.

With increased access to guns, cars, and drugs, female gang members have discovered that they need not be dependent on male gang members and the females are getting to be just like the men. And some don't care who they shoot. Despite the young women's increasing criminal activities, shootings by girl gang members are still rare, but they happen. Mexican girl gang members operate much like the male members and they are similar in almost every aspect to the male members and like the Black females, they get involved in all aspects of gang crime from street fights to committing felonies, they sell drugs, or some become the carriers of drugs for the males.

Today it is not uncommon to read in the newspapers of females involved in drive-by shootings. In the mean time the law enforcement community is having a difficult time addressing the girl gang problem because they don't have the basic knowledge or techniques to address this female problem.

The females work together with the male gang members and often operate as a team and they are becoming less subservient to the males as they were in the past. The girls are used to drive the cars because they are less suspicious and are not recognized by rivals, or the police. In the mean time the male member is free to shoot someone and often hide in the back seat until the actual shooting takes place, by the male. The Latin girls, like the black girls, are used to transport drugs, known as carriers because they look less suspicious and often do it cheaper than black girls, or they do it to obtain drugs for themselves and they do abuse drugs as do the Black girls, especially marijuana, heroin and cocaine.

The Latina gang members look and act like girls, they are the girls males use to hold their weapons and drugs because they don't look like gang members, They can also be used to buy guns due to their clean arrest records and if the guns are found in a gang members hands, the girls can claim that the guns were stolen and the police believe them because they don't look suspicious. They are very convincing when creating an alibi for the males and they also testify to the alibi in court. That doesn't mean that the "girls" are not violent if they need to be.

Latinas sometimes wear the same uniform or clothing as the males do including the colors red and blue. They prefer to wear pants and they seldom wear dresses, their hair is long, full, and sometimes dyed blonde or red. Their body tattoos may be crucifixes and rosaries on their chest or backs and that sends the message that they will die for their neighborhood or barrio. If they are schoolgirls they may wear the actual crucifixes and rosaries.

BLACK FEMALE GANG MEMEBERS

Black female gang members are into money sex and drug trafficking, and the females have specific jobs. The lesbians are more involved in violent crimes, just like the males and they are expected to defend themselves just like the males do. One could say that they are treated almost like males. The Black female gang members, much like the Latino girls, look and act like girls, they are the girls males use to hold their weapons and drugs because they don't look like gang members, They can also be used to buy guns due to their clean arrest records and if the guns are found in a gang members hands, the girls can claim that the guns were stolen and the police believe them because they don't look suspicious. They are very convincing when creating an alibi for the males and they also testify to the alibi in court. That doesn't mean that the "girls" are not violent if they need to be.

Consequently, Black, and Latina girls ought to be treated just like the hard-core male gang members. The Black females wear individual styles of clothing from each other. But some of the girls dress similar to the males, making it difficult to tell the males and females apart. However, this is an extreme case and the females will just dress in ordinary clothes, but they will wear red or blue depending on the gang they belong to and they may even paint their finger nails in these colors. Black female gang members are mostly into money, sex, and drug trafficking, and they have specific jobs with in the gang structure.

ASIAN FEMALE GANG MEMBERS

The Asian girl gang members initially began their own gangs because they were frustrated with the male members and also because they wanted to be liberated and involved in their own criminal activities. Perhaps they wanted liberation to overcome much of the subservient upbringing in the native culture and homeland. Filipino and Vietnamese females have also begun to operate independent from the male counter-parts. However, the Korean females associate with male gang members, but it is not known if the females are active gang members. Along with the stereotypical subservient Asian "China Doll" there are South East Asians cultural marriage customs causing some of these girls to run away from home. For instance Hmong girls may be required to marry at a much early age.

Consequently, most of the Asian females are "runaways" who run away as young as 12 to 13 years of age. Because they are on their own, there strongest motivation is survival and they can and will commit any crime in order to survive. The Asian females are mostly used for easy entry into homes because Asian gangs are basically involved in property crimes. Recently some of the Asian males have raped young innocent girls and then turned them into prostitutes.

Therefore, Asian females are a major concern to law enforcement and the school sites. The females have adopted the characteristics of the Latin girl gang members including their hair and makeup and will dress differently than non-gang members. They tend to favor short black skirts, tops, spiked high heels, and black stockings. However, whatever they wear will give the appearance that they are young and innocent to the average person, such as educators. Consequently, they are often not bothered by police nor understood by school administrators.

THE GANG STRUCTURES

Recently newspapers have been reporting that crime is on the rise and police don't seem to know why. One answer could be because incarcerated gang members have now been paroled and are continuing the life style they had before they went to prison. Another answer could be that the middle school students have now graduated high school and are now gang members. As a community and as teachers we need to understand that the hard-core Latino gangs are structured like the military, which means they are, or were well organized. Being well organized may not be so any longer except maybe in the urban areas in the state of California. The following pages show this structure.

THE GENERALS

The Mexican mafia (sureños) and la familia (norteños) are the hard-core gang leaders, or the generals who are be in prison for life, but they distribute their orders with paroled gang members, to gang members on the outside, or on the street.

THE OFFICERS (PAROLEES)

They communicate the general's orders to the members outside of prison.

THE SOLDIERS

The street gang members and dope dealers and can be people not yet in prison. However, they often are recruited in the grade school, middle school, and the high school students who are the military cadets. They can also be called the wanna-bee's who emulate the gang members.

THE GANG MEMBERS

Some may be in juvenile hall and many gang members may view prison as a graduate university. Gang members often consider the prison, a graduate school for gang members. Many of the gang members want to graduate and go to college, which is what they call the prison, so that they can study under the "big guys," or the big Chingones who are known as the professors of the Mexican Mafia and La Familia gang leaders, who are in prison. In prison they learn the dos and don'ts of the "street" so that they don't return to the prison because they are not good to the gang for selling drugs if they return to prison with a life sentence. As in real life, it is all about economics.

Consequently, putting youngsters in jail is their promotion to higher education or graduate school. Some gang members do not view going to prison as a punishment, they view it, as it is a reward! That is what they want! What does this say about building more prisons? These prisons are also known as "Penn State University."

AFRICAN AMERICAN GANGS

The origin of Black gangs in California originated in the 1920s in Los Angeles. They were known as the "Boozies" who were primarily involved in street crime. Between 1940 and 1960 more Black gangs were formed and inter-gang rivalry developed. In the early 1970's the Crips were formed in Los Angeles area and Anti-Crips emerged shortly after and became known as "The Bloods". The Bloods and the Crips originated in the cities of Compton and Watts of south Los Angeles, and the Willow brook area Southeast of LA in the late 1960s. From there they scattered into other parts of the LA area. For instance the Bloods, such as the Bounty Hunters, Brims, and Denver Lanes, spread throughout LA County.

The Crips gangs formed in the same way as the Bloods. They were the originals. As the Crips grew they formed gangs such as Santana Block Crips, 62 east Coast Crips, and many more. Because Latin gang members are very artistic and experienced, many Black gang members have Latinos paint their tattoos. These tattoos are on their arms and upper torso. Black gangs actually learned how to "gang bang" from Latino gangs because the Latin groups had been into gangs, around LA, long before the Black gangs started forming.

The black guerrilla family is a prison gang that is aligned with the Nuestra Familia gang. Philosophically it is the most radical and only Blacks can join them. It can be politically motivated and is known to assault prison staff. The folk and people nations gang, known as the "nations," are gang groups that are based in Chicago and they originated in the 1980's within the prison system. They formed for protection from other coalitions and this alliance formed as two groups called "Folks" and "People." However, SOME alliances are not based on race alone, like other traditional gangs. Gang alliances are taken from the streets of Chicago and are now the bases for bitter rivalry between the Folks and the People gangs.

There are many street gangs, but each is aligned with the Folks or People. The alliance of the folk and people are now known as "Nations." The "People" gangs use identifiers, such as symbols, on the left side of the body:

1. Earring worn on left side
2. Pant leg rolled up on left side
3. Cap tilted to the left
4. The hand sign is thrown toward the left shoulder
5. Members may fold arms in a manner that will point to their left.

Other symbols are:

1. Five point star (origin: Blackstone Rangers, Black gang)
2. Five pointed crown
3. Pitch forks drawn upside down (shows disrespect to Folk Nation)
4. Top hat
5. Cane
6. Triangle with sun top inside
7. The number five
8. Their colors are Black or Red

THE FOLKS GANG USE IDENTIFIERS AS SYMBOLS ON THE RIGHT SIDE OF THEIR BODY:

1. Six stars
2. Heart
3. Pitch forks pointed up
4. Crown with rounded edges
5. The number 6
6. Heart with wings
7. Pointed tail

Their colors are Blue and Black

The Folks and People gangs developed terms, originally in prison where no identifiers are allowed. Allegiances to the gang are "representing" is the term used to indicate allegiance to the Folks or People. but the west coast uses the term "claiming." The leadership is normally given to the founder of the gang and the structure is the leader and core members. The levels of the leadership are, the "hard-core gang members."

They have unwavering loyalty to the gang. The "associates" will leave the gang loyalty when in need of self-preservation. The "fringe" members allow outside activities to influence loyalty to the gang. And finally, the "outsiders" usually join in their late teens just to make money. Their activities are mostly criminal. These activities range from car thefts, to organized drug sales and on to murder. Their graffiti will contain symbols of the nation. Insults or challenges can be given by drawing the rival gang's graffiti upside down, or by marking or crossing out the rival's gang graffiti. The graffiti shows presence of a gang as well as turf boundaries. The Black gangs also have structures and similar things that were said about the Latino gang structure, Following is a comparison to the Latino gang member structure.

"THE GANGSTER DISCIPLES HIERARCHY IN CHICAGO"

CHAIRMAN OF THE BOARD

Incarcerated members who control the gang's operations through two boards of Directors

BOARD OF DIRECTORS	BOARD OF DIRECTORS
(In prison)	(Out on the streets)
Controls incarcerated member's Operations	Controls street member's operations

GOVERNORS

Controls drug trafficking operations

REGENTS

Supplies drugs and selling locations for the members

COORDINATORS

Distribute drugs to dealers and collects the profits for the top leaders.

ENFORCERS

Mete out violations ranging from beatings and perhaps death for members that disobey gang rules.

SHORTIES

Young rank and file members who sell the drugs on the street and who guard their territory.

An example of why the leadership has such an easy time recruiting and holding on to gang members, outside of prisons, is explained in an article by "The Christian Science Monitor," Boston Mass, 1996, "A boy's one Day in a Gang." The article covers more information than one day, and has-been taken or paraphrased to fit the ideas of this book,

At age 13, Greg obediently stood security watch for the gang's turf for $50 a day. At age 14, he went to jail for shooting a rival in the back to protect his gang. At age 16, with a beeper on him he shows up on schedule to sell drugs for the gang. Being late will bring a fine, a "violation," or a brutal beating by his gang's enforcers. Are you searching brother? I got it. I got the rock (crack cocaine). I got the boy (heroin)." After a few hours on the job, Greg has sold $500. The gang takes $350 and gives Greg $150, based on a 70-30 split. This has happened in Chicago, but it can happen anywhere in our communities. Most gangs operate in similar situations, but may vary from location to location.

One could say that there is an invisible infrastructure where billions of dollars are a hidden economy that could fund many drug programs. If we compared the American drug situation to European countries, such as The Netherlands, where they tax the drugs that are under governmental control. But they think that the United States is losing billions of dollars generated by drug sales. Whereas in the Netherlands use the tax on drugs for social programs. Whereas in Netherlands has a tax base from the sale of drugs in their country. In the United States, the "war on drugs" could be totally financed by taxing the illegal drugs that enter the United States. Does this mean that the author advocated the sale or use of drugs? No, he merely advises that the American Government take a realistic view upon the war on drugs. If we as a nation understand that as long as there is a demand, there will be a supply.

The gang's operations are also well organized into networks in a Mafia-like structure, which is also like a military structure. It is a multi-million dollar business that stretches into all areas of America. The business is propelled by profit-hungry drug dealers and craving addicts. It is a "supply and demand" business. Unfortunately, our government focuses on the supply side and not on the demand side of this business. Is it any wonder that many people say that our drug war is a losing proposition?

As long as someone craves anything, there will be a supply. If we concentrated on the demand side, as is in some European countries, perhaps our war on drugs could be won. Most Black gangs are incredibly well disciplined and trained by intelligent leaders. The Crips and the Bloods are like roaming bands of drug dealers who seem to have no leaders. Is this why maybe we don't hear about these two gangs any more?

The Mexican Mafia (sureños and the Familia (norteños) are also well organized. However, they seem to be declining in organization and the "old timers are losing control of many street youth gangs.

WHAT FORMER UNITED STATES ATTORNEY GENERAL JANET RENO HAS SAID ABOUT GANGS

Gang violence has spread to every corner of America. She also stated that there are an estimated 650,000-gang members, and 25,000 gangs nationwide. Gangs are not what we may think it is. Our view, without information presents us a picture of a kid that shows gang membership in dress and appearance. But often we are wrong in our perceptions. The gang leaders are very strict and prohibit other members from using addictive drugs, gambling on credit, engaging in homosexual rape, being a bad sport, and stealing from or disrespecting other gang members. All this comes from the experiences of the gang leadership in prison. Their membership, personal cleanliness, and exercise are also required. (Many of them have been ripped off or raped in prison so they discourage these type activities, the author's entry). The picture we may have in our mind about gang members is not based on reality because the reality is that the leaders continue to control their gang's activities from prison. We may think that the members outside of prison are the ones to be feared, but in actuality, it is the ones inside that are to be feared because they give the orders of who dies and who lives, whether you are a gang member or not; if you interfere with their operations.

MORE ABOUT GANGS IN GENERAL

Colors are very important to gang members. The Crips use, or wear items using the color blue. The anti Crips use, or wear items using the color red, the use of rags, bandanas, or headscarfs to show colors. The Blood-Piru-Cuzz-Crip, are heavily involved in drug trade and adopted many Latino gang characteristics. Most crimes are against each other for protection of drug turfs. In L. A., the Crips are located west of Central LA and the Bloods are located east of Central LA.

1. Structure-loose knit, except in Chicago
2. Leadership -fluctuates-usually led by founders
3. Structure influenced by models of Latino gangs including the drug trade.
4. The Black gangs are leaving LA because of the stability of Latino gangs. Therefore, very few operate in L.A. right now and the Latino gangs are flourishing.

WHITE SKIN HEADS

Usually White youth do not join gangs and they express their delinquent behavior individually and not within a gang per se. When they do join a gang it will most likely be with other ethnic gangs, but certainly not Black gangs. However, some whites did become involved in the "Skinhead movement in the 1960s and formed ties with the KKK, Nazi Party, and other militant racist groups.

The Skinheads normally come from the same type environment, as do the other ethnic gangs. And like the other ethnic gangs, the group they join becomes their surrogate family. Of course hate crime against minorities is common in the racist Skin Head movement. This group is identified by various names, and their name, Skinhead, was derived from their habit of shaving their head, probably because they did not want their hair pulled when they were involved in street fights.

Of the two types of Skinheads the one addressed here is another racist group and they are known as "White Pride", White Power, White supremacy, or Nazi Skins. However, they are usually unorganized, and small in numbers compared the ethnic gangs. They are mostly white males and females. They have shaved heads and are involved with heavy racist rock bands. They also use tattoos and graffiti. They hate Jews, Blacks, Asians, Latinos, and homosexuals. They are involved with the Aryan Nation, White Aryan Resistance, White student Union and the Aryan Youth movement.

Their criminal activities are robbery, vandalism, auto theft, possession of illegal weapons, explosives, and assault with deadly weapons, more over, they commit crimes, thrill killings, and murder. Other information is as follows:

1. Evolved from Punk/Stoner groups
2. They are into White Power SWP, Nazi, and Anti Minority groups
3. Violent/Anti-Establishment and are into Heavy metal music
4. Their mental Health problems are unstable, and may feel powerless.

These people practice anarchy and also abuse drugs. They are also into racial intimidation, violence and anti-establishment, such as schools and governmental policies

ASIAN GANGS IN GENERAL

Each Asian group has a different culture and language, but many have assimilated with established American street gangs. They have language problems in interpretation and translation. They have police problems because in many of these countries the police are crooked and it is the lowest form of employment, therefore, the citizens do not respect police. Their victims usually are other Asians and often their own racial group.

Consequently, they commit residential and business robberies and run protection rackets. They assault, steal autos, intimidate witnesses and often commit murder. They usually deal with traffic in narcotics, such opium and morphine.

Each Asian gang has it's own unique characteristics. However, the average age is between 16 and 25. But, there may be some as young as 10 years old. Asians do not have tattoos painted on their body because they consider this practice as degrading. However, cigarette burns or other marks that show "machismo" will be displayed on their hands, wrists, fore arms, or lower legs.

THE CHINESE

Their crimes are extortion, gambling robbery and rape. Most crimes are committed against the wealthy Asians. They import heroin, they are involved in alien smuggling, prostitution and drug abuse. The ethnic Chinese from Asia are involved in many criminal activities, they are ruthless, involved in residential robberies, medical and insurance fraud and are also into car thefts and extortion and their average age is between 18-25 year and are led by "godfather like individuals." Moreover:

A. They are the outgrowth of the old time Tong Organizations.
B. The Wah Ching (young youth) established in the mid-sixties and are mostly born in Hong Kong.
C. The Wah Ching eventually split and formed a new group called Yu Li.
D. Then Joe Fong left the Yu Li to form the Joe Boys.
E. The Viet Ching, the most recent group formed by the Vietnam Chinese and has attempted to challenge the Wah Ching gang.
F. Their style of killing is brutal, and believes in torturing the victims before they are killed.

KOREAN GANGS

Their ages are 13-30 years old and most are foreign born. Their criminal activities are within the Korean communities in the form of extortion, business and residential robberies. They are also into opium and morphine production, and smuggling of Southeast Asian heroin in to the United States. They are organized and recruit street gang members. They have street gangs as well as international, and national gang affiliations.

These gangs do not claim turf and members will travel wherever necessary to make money. Rival Asian gang members will work together for a specific crime, split the proceeds, and then become rivals again. The three gangs in Los Angeles are known as Korean Killers, American Burger Boys, and South Bay Killers and they will use Korean Yellow pages to select victims. They are very cooperative with the police while detained.

VIETNAMESE GANGS

Associate primarily with Chinese gangs or Viet Ching. There are three Vietnamese gangs and are called Pink Nights, Dragon Boys and the Pomona Boys and use three names to avoid identification, birth, school and neighborhood

LAOTIAN GANGS   35

There are many gang members in the San Joaquin Valley of California and other states. However, identifying them is difficult because not much research has been conducted about them. The Laotian gangs are the following ethnic groups found in Laos They are the Hmong, the Lao, and the Mien.

However, it is known that in the San Joaquin Valley of California that the Cambodian, Lao, Hmong, and Mien gangs do exist. The Cambodians are not from Laos, but they are included with this group because not much is known about Cambodian gang members. In many large cities the Southeast Asian gangs emulate violence similar to that of their war-torn childhood homes, although current Asian gangs are now first generation Americans and may not remember their homeland. Fears of Asian residents have been fanned by reports of gang rampages in which youth, family members, and strangers were maimed or killed.

Public schools figure prominently among the locations of gang violence. Not only are they the site for rival gang conflicts, but also their wanton violence and extortion intimidate teachers with demands for higher-grade changes and with sexual assaults. But gangs are not all the same, even if they are of the same ethnic group, the same socioeconomic and cultural background. (A. James Schwartz, Oct. 1998). An important note about the Asians is that most seldom participate in "drive-by" shootings in their own hometown.

The Asian refugees such as the Hmong, Mien, or Lao may have become gang members in the refugee camps of Thailand and may have become gang members for protection and assuming some sort of power in the strange land. Therefore, of the Asians may have been "trained" into the gang life style in their country of origin before they arrived in the United States. It ought to be remembered that many Laotians were soldiers, for the United States, as young as 12 years old. Consequently, they were well prepared to transition into gangs.

When there is a need to eliminate a rival gang member, or any other considered the enemy they have someone from out of town (one of their "hommies") to do the shooting. The imported shooter usually completes the job then returns to his hometown, which can be quite a distance from where the shooting took place. Mean while the police may be looking for the shooter where the shooting took place, but the shooter has gone back to his hometown. Little by little some local police are learning to address this problem and this type of violence

SUMMARY ABOUT GANGS

It ought to be remembered that gangs have been with s since the beginning of organized society. Gang violence is a community problem that requires a multi-agency, community based solutions, and this includes the schools and parents. It needs to be understood that the gang problem is a community problem and are not exclusively a police or school problem. Elected officials need to be involved in all these problems because the incarceration and suppression strategies alone will not solve the American gang problem no more than the war on drugs has solved the drug problem. Therefore, community organizations, outreach programs, and vocational training programs are also required to effectively treat and prevent gang problems.

Prevention should be the future focus of the drug war because as long as there are users there will be drugs. Much of the gang activity is driven by the control of members, neighborhoods, turf and manipulation of others. Gangs capitalize on the natural fear of gangs by community members. However, (as was stated before) in Los Angeles today there is less graffiti and drive-bys were discouraged because the Mafia prisoners dictated it. This has not affected the rural areas because there is now more graffiti in smaller towns and cities than in Los Angeles.

However, keep it in mind that what was a problem in the past may not be the same problem today. Combating the gang phenomenon is a task for all of society and we all need to be involved. But educators, who are in the battlefield of the war on drugs can go far in deterring this phenomenon by simply treating all students with dignity and respect in the classroom. The classroom is the first place where students can be motivated to stay away from gangs, or change negative to positive behaviors. As the statistics have shown above, "the gang members consider an education as a worth while endeavor."

CHAPTER 3

INFORMATION FOR TEACHERS:
EDUCATION CAN PREVENT GANG INVOLVEMENT

Anchee Min, author of Becoming Madame Mao, in an article titled "Education saves lives," in USA Weekend page 4, August 6, 2000. In the same article she mentioned the following: "If you want to make a beast out of human being(s) take away education ... education... provides a sense of self and a sense of compassion for the value of human lives." The author of this book is a former teacher trainer at a university and feels the same as Ms. Min and he paraphrases her by saying, "I am embarrassed when given credit for inspiring new teachers and making a difference." However, compared to teachers, who face the battlefield everyday, the author feels that his efforts are minimal.

The following information is stated again because it may be useful to the parents and teachers as they conduct the business of teaching children. Currently, in the schools there are two Latino gangs called the Mexican Mafia, or Sureños and another gang known as La Familia, or "Norteños". The author uses the Latino gangs as examples but everyone needs to understand that most ethnic groups have gangs, as well as the White community. Parents and teachers ought to learn a few things about gangs at home and in the classroom, especially how non-verbal communication is used by gang members such as flashing gang signs (hand signs) because these signs identifies the user with a specific gang. However, the author must stress that other ethnic groups in the America are not free of gang membership.

Here the author presents two examples to stress the need to understand the students in the schoolrooms:

In the spring of 2002 the author was supervising a student teacher in a very small town in Merced County. California. While he was observing the student teacher, he and the "master teacher" I saw a male 4th grader flashing a sign, and the teacher asked the student supervisor if it was a gang signal and the author said' "yes." Then the teacher wanted to know how the supervisor knew this? The author told the master teacher, "the student flashed three fingers on his chest and that meant that the student was a sureño (Southern wanna bee gang member). Then the teacher was told that the number three is used to denote number 13, which is the 13th letter of the alphabet and that it meant the thirteenth letter of the alphabet which is "M". The "M" means" Mexican Mafia" who are also known as "sureños". The master teacher then asked, "if he should refer the student to the principle or the on site police resource officer." The author told the master teacher, "neither because both of these individuals are more interested in punishment and what is needed are prevention strategies at this grade level because prevention is very effective in keeping students from becoming hard core gang members."

Consequently, anyone who understands the gang culture that the student flashing three fingers, would know something about the student. But unfortunately, few teachers know or have learned anything about this and they may, some day get assaulted. The teacher in this example is a veteran teacher of many years in the classroom, but the master teacher probably entered the profession before gang activity became as serious as it is in these modern times. But are the new teachers better off? No! They have not learned about gangs either. In fact the student teacher, who was being supervised was in shock when she heard the discussion because she was going to teach in the school where she was doing her student teaching, which is located in her hometown, where this school is located.

After her initial shock she asked, "Why was I not taught this at the university?" And the supervisor answered her, "I don't know, but I seem to be the only professor that teaches about gangs in the teacher training program and my other colleagues don't because they don't seem to have the time, or don't know about gangs in the classroom.

We have to learn about what is happening in the real world and then make time to teach the real world of teaching because the students they will be teaching in the real world." The Master teacher agreed and he wished that all new teachers would possess this knowledge and he also said that he wished that he knew more about gangs to help him become a better teacher. In the second example the following occurred:

One day, the author was visiting a middle school and as he walked around the school grounds he came upon an empty Pepsi Cola container or can that was slightly dented on one side with a pinhole through the dent. As he looked at it, he knew immediately that this Pepsi can was used as a pipe to smoke dope (by the way, any soft drink aluminum can, can be used). He took the can to the principle and showed it to her then asked her, "do you know what this is?" She told him, "It is a Pepsi can and a group of our students meet each day, far removed from the office, to drink their Pepsi, and she said, "they are good kids and seldom caused problems, or bothered anyone and are peaceful in class." The author said to himself, "of course they're peaceful, they are high on drugs." However, the principal was upset because the kids had not placed the can in the proper disposal container. The author then told her about how the can was used to smoke dope and she couldn't believe it, but she thanked the author as he left the school site and knowing that she probably didn't believe him because he is a 73-year-old man who couldn't possibly know about gangs and drugs. The 73-year-old man has learned much about this from his grandson named Dominic. Did the principle address the drug problem? Who knows, but she is not alone because many educators would rather deny that anything like this would happen in their schools because they have not been taught about gangs and drugs. Educators need to be observant of student's actions and behaviors in school because students are very smart and can fool adults very easily.

Many youths in gangs often do not feel alienated from the school objectives and many of them like school and love to learn. However, they don't participate, or are not encouraged to participate in student governance, and they view teachers negatively. They also believe that as students, they do not get the academic grades they deserve and that teachers do not give them extra help when needed. They also believe that they are just passed to a higher grade just to get rid of them. On the other hand it does not help the schools or teachers, if they don't learn about gangs and how to address the gang problem beginning in the third or fourth grades.

Many of the students that join gangs suffer from low self-esteem because they lack success, at home and in school. As soon as they join a gang they have immediate success, acceptance, and develop a good self-esteem while they are learning, even if adults see this as a negative behavior. Educators can keep students from becoming gang members if they are helped to succeed in school and provide a positive self-esteem. Educators ought to focus on the student instead of the gang clothing and stop stereotyping the students who may just need additional help in the classroom.

The clothing is not the problem because focusing on clothing is like focusing on the hole rather than on the "donut." The inmates in a prison all wear the same type clothing usually, blue jeans and light chambray shirts, and this has not deterred gang communication within the prison. Gang members are indeed very intelligent.

There is a gang culture, and educators need to learn what the culture is. Administrators and teachers often focus on ethnic minorities and European cultures, but they know very little about the gang culture. Consequently, there is little communication between the teacher and the gang members. Teachers and educators should also know that Latinos and Southeast Asian students often replace their native culture with that of the gang culture. That is why we have a difficult time understanding how these minority students change and they no longer show respect for their parents, teachers, and other authority figures in their community.

However, gang members are committed to the community, and this is something that educators can focus on. Gang delinquency is deviant behavior without positive values to achieve "successful goals." Why? They now see their parents as "losers" who work for minimum wages and in dead-end jobs. They view the schools as a waste of time and they feel that with gang membership they can sell drugs which is a way out of poverty and misery. Many have asked gang members, "You will probably die before you are 20 years old. Aren't you afraid to die?"

Their reasoning is, "I would rather die young and rich, than to live one hundred years like my mom and dad!" It is difficult to argue with this logic. They also see that the schools practice a double stand in terms of grading practices. As students they also want high educational standards, instead of a "watered down" standards. They also want high expectations and fairness from teachers and in the delivery of educational, objectives and grades. If these issues are not addressed there will be a continuation and expansion of gang membership in the schools!

"Once a gang member, always a gang member." Currently, the only way out of gangs is extremely difficult and often the prize for leaving a gang is death! Therefore, educators could convince a gang member to "leave the gang," but then they may be signing their death warrant. Can any of us live with that?

However, if we know or understand the gang culture we would know that the only way out of gangs for them is to help them set priorities, such as "a mother raising a baby or a father making a life for his family." More importantly, to get a college degree, then they are allowed to just "fade out" of the gang, but they still remain a member of the gang, but are left alone as long as they do not join another gang. Sometimes, after they fade out, the gang leadership may still test them by asking them to participate in gang and illegal activities, and usually if the member agrees, he or she is told to stay home and study! However, keeping them away from gangs to begin with is much more preferable and educators can do this by "teaching the kids with a fair and equitable manner and with a caring attitude." Many students would not join or remain in gangs to begin with if teachers would provide them with a solid education.

Consequently, this is where teachers, come in. We cannot expect a student to come from a dysfunctional home into a perceived dysfunctional classroom, due to a teacher's unfamiliarity with the gang culture, or ethnic minorities. Teachers need to make the classroom a home where these young people can feel safe. After all they could become scientists, or mathematicians. However, in all preventive efforts the parents must be included in the war against drugs and everyone must share part of the blame for not keeping kids away from drugs and gang membership.

Let us also remember that gang membership is not confined to the poverty inner-city youngsters only and that gang members who become professionals do not break ties with their gang affiliations. Remember, "once a gang member, always a gang member." There are many professionals that are still gang members. For instance, one well known gang member is a professional football player in a well-known football team, who on one Sunday caught five passes ran for 106 yards and 2 touch downs. Yet he often entered the dressing room wearing the color red on his person and flashing hand signs. This football player still has an allegiance to the Swan Family Bloods of South Central Los Angeles. These professionals are often "heroes" to the gang members we are trying to teach!

Teenagers in far too many places in America are dying - brutally, unnecessarily, prematurely, and in senseless moments each year in America. In 1992 alone, the number totaled more than 7,000. Behind these deaths is a jumble of twisted emotions and warped values, unbridled anger, vengeance, cold-hearted retribution, misplaced loyalty, and false bravado that confound psychologists, schoolteachers, social workers, probation officers, and law enforcement agencies. Some have called these youth "The young and the ruthless".

Why this phenomenon? It is not only the "feel good society" that is at fault, but we must also hold the mass media accountable. Prevention is very possible if society and teachers understand the gang culture

WHAT THE AMERICAN PSYCHOLOGICAL ASSOCIATION (APA) says about this?

The average child is exposed to 8,000 television murders and more than 100,000 other violent acts by the time they enter seventh grade. Saturday morning programming for children is far worse, with 20 to 25 violent acts per hour. There is no doubt that higher levels of viewing violence on TV are correlated with increased acceptance of aggressive attitudes and increased aggressive behavior. More importantly, youngsters who see their days as numbered, or who see no future-and certainly not a bright one-what is the point of staying in school, practicing safe sex, and avoiding drugs?

To these youngsters, killing is acceptable because they see it on TV every day and night and killing is glamorized. Unfortunately, TV is often used as a "baby sitter" for working mothers. However, teachers and parents ought to spend a couple of hours one Saturday morning watching TV with their young children and they will probably be horrified at what is shown on "Kids Programs. The author is convinced that schools have a great role to play in ensuring that students receive the help that they need at the first sign that the students are slipping behind academically. Schools need not wait until a violent act occurs. Educators must also review what programs are vital and what programs perpetuate the problem. For instance, some studies have noted that students that participate in DARE tend to abuse drugs more than those students that have not participated in the program. Uniforms are often seen as a deterrent to gang membership, but it does not, as was shown above, but needs to be reiterated here.

The author was part of an accreditation team for a high school program at the Sierra Conservation Camp... a California adult prison in Jamestown California. The uniform for prisoners is jeans and denim shirts. Yet Latino gang members passed messages to one another by using a Rosary, they hand made in their cells, and how they hang out of their rear pockets, or belt loop and the number and manner of how the beads hung out of their pocket send messages to their "homies." The prisoners are very smart and so are the K-12 students when forced them to wear uniforms, they find ways to communicate with their "homies. In other words, as was said before, looking at uniforms to deter gangs is like looking at "the hole instead of the donut" especially because they talk to each other all day long.

The real key to deter gang membership is an excellent, and fair education, for all students without double standards in the classroom. If teachers do not change the way they deliver instruction and how they relate to students that they all their students are accepted in positive ways, then ten percent of schoolteachers will probably be violently assaulted during their career by one of their students.

Consequently, critical to preventing violence in the schools is support for teachers' efforts in addressing discipline problems. Teachers are on the front line every day and are responsible for discipline problems. Therefore, it is extremely important that teachers receive total support from site and central office administrators.

Yet there are some administrators who complain that the teachers are lax in discipline rules. Mean while the teachers complain that the administrators do not support them when they refer students for disruptive or violent behavior. Yes teachers need to be consistent in enforcement of school rules related to non-acceptable behavior. And administrators need to provide teachers and other staff members with the assurance that violent students will be dealt with firmly, consistently, and swiftly.

Moreover, teachers must also receive support when they try to maintain an orderly classroom. There is nothing more discouraging to a teacher than sending disruptive students to the office and a few minutes later the student is back in the classroom bragging that going "to the office was no big deal because they were not punished!" The teachers must know that they have total support from administrators, the school board, and yes, even the parents. As has been stated more than once, "some school personnel, and society are in denial that there is a gang problem in the schools. It is time to bring this problem to the forefront to better address it.

However, recognizing and accepting that a gang problem exists in the schools of today then educators may be accepting of the idea and finally decide that a need for changes in the schools are needed. Then critical steps can be taken to reduce or eliminate gang and school violence in the schools. However, change is a process that requires commitment from all people involved in the process of education, which includes the district top administrators and school boards.

In the K-6 classrooms most of the students are "wanna bee" members. This means that they are still not hard-core gang members, but may socialize with hard-core members because they want to be hard-core some day. This is the place where the schools have the opportunity to stop the gang cycle. In the 7-12 classrooms it may too late because they may already be hard-core, but there is still an opportunity to stop the vicious cycle of gangs in the K-12 schools. Following are some suggestions that schools need to apply when addressing the gang issue in schools and is summary of what has been stated before:

1. Educators can keep students from becoming gang members if they help students succeed in school and also provide strategies that foster positive self-esteem. Educators ought to focus on the student instead of the "gang clothing." In the K-5 schools the students are wanna bee's and not yet hard-core gang members and focusing on the gang clothing just leads to stereotypes of the kids.

2. Gang membership does create a gang culture, and educators need to learn about their culture. We often concentrate on cultures of ethnic minorities, but we know very little about the gang culture. Quite often Latinos and Southeast Asians replace their home culture with the gang culture and that is why teachers often have a difficult time understanding how they show little respect for their parents and teachers. Educators often learn the home culture that is quite different from the gang culture and they are unprepared for the subtle changes of culture the longer the "new immigrants" reside in the United States.

3. Gang members remain committed to the community, and this is something that educators can focus on, remembering that their community is their turf.

4. Gang delinquency is deviant behavior that lacks positive values to achieve successful goals because they see their parents as losers. They also view the schools as a waste of time. They feel that selling drugs is a way out of poverty and misery. They often also say that the school's practice a double standard in terms of assignments and grading practices. They desire high educational

standards coupled with high expectations and fairness in the delivery of grades and delivery of the curriculum. Many of them have indicated that they also want a college education.

HOW GANG MEMBERS VIEW EDUCATION

Almost 92% expected to complete high school. When asked how far they think they will go in school, 22% said Jr. College, 23% said a four -year college, and 8% graduate studies. Their occupational aspirations are unexpectedly high as well; and one-third wanted professional jobs and almost 40% wanted white-collar jobs. It was found that these youth were not alienated from the school objectives, but many stated they were alienated from school itself. They don't participate, or are not encouraged to participate in student governance, and they viewed teachers negatively, because the students do not usually get grades that they believed they deserved and teachers do not give them extra help when needed. This is a double standard that many teachers practice because they don't understand the damage they are causing.

Sadly, 1/2 of the gang members could not name an in-school adult to whom they could go to with personal, social, or academic problems, and more gang members than others perceived school racial and ethnic relations as poor. Over 1/2 agree that minorities are not treated fairly; and that people of different race or ethnicity do not get along well in school, and that school rules are not applied uniformly.

THE MASS MEDIA

The Merced Sun Star has reported

Merced California is a small city of over 67,000 Population in the California San Joaquin Valley. Merced is the largest city in the county; however, it has about 70 gangs, which is equal to Fresno County, a much larger county. Violence is increasing and officials don't understand why, although they believe that most violence is gang related. The newly elected County Sheriff, stated, "I don't know if (recent shooting) it is an increase in gang activity or violence in general."

The most recent shootings have been by the Asian gangs, such as the Men of Destruction (MOD). The MOD members exist in Minnesota and throughout California and in cities like Modesto, Merced, Sacramento, and San Francisco. Along with the MODs, there is the True Blue and the Oriental LOCS and they are all rivals in the small cities of California.

According to a Merced City Police, Sgt, "violent crimes have been increasing," and he doesn't know which gangs are committing the most violent crimes, but there has been an increase of Asian and Hispanic gangs.

However, he stressed, "violence" is a problem with all gangs including Asian, Caucasian, Black gangs. All the people that were interviewed said that the gang problem is a COMMUNITY problem and that every one needs to be involved if this problem is to be addressed. The city police Chief, stated, "Crime is not just a police problem. It is a community problem. People just need to be involved in crime prevention."

The author maintains that many students would not join or remain in gangs, whose business is the drug trade, if they were provide with a solid education because some gang members do desire a college degree. The Police Chief of Merced also states, "this is a community problem," and the author agrees. Moreover, in schools, education is their focus and throughout this book the author stresses, "it is indeed a community problem" and not just a problem for law enforcement and education. The schools are under the leadership of community people that are elected by the community. Therefore, the community must be involved in learning about gangs in the schools.

Two suggestions for beginning educators are listed as follows:

1. Special focus should be placed on improved K-12 education, employment training, and job placement for all students. Studies have shown that the schools are the first area of gang membership or prevention. Usually the candidates for gang membership are those students that are quiet or are seldom called on, have little respect from the teacher and that the dominant culture students are the favorites. Some minority students feel that a "White student can misbehave 2 or 3 times before they are punished," whereas a minority student behaves just once and they are punished. They also feel they are under a microscope and that they must behave 100 percent of the time. This is undue pressure to minority students that want to learn, but feel they need to behave 100 percent of the time and this detracts from the learning process. Whether this is true or not, the issue is, if minority students feel this way then it is negative learning.

2. Focus on individual youth behavior and value changes. Teachers, can channel the student's intelligence in positive ways and make them positive contributors to society. Heroin has made a come back, killing some 4,000 people a year. Educators will have to address these issues, and find the means that can compete with the drug income that "children" can earn, sometimes as much as $200 a day.

What is listed above can be a beginning for educators. Educators simply cannot expect a student to come from a dysfunctional home to a perceived dysfunctional classroom and instead make the classroom a home where these young people can feel safe and then they can learn to be scientists, mathematicians, or plumbers. In all the community's efforts the parents must be included in the war against drugs school violence and everyone must share part of the blame and responsibility.

What Gang members have in common is: (1) they scored higher on measures on the Use of language other than English. (2) Their friends don't like school, (3)-peer deviance and physical insecurity while in school, (4) they have low self-concept in academics, and a positive racial-ethnic relations in school. Never – the - less, gang members valued the schools academic program.

DO'S AND DON'TS IN RELATION TO GANG PREVENTION IN THE CLASSROOM

DO'S

1. Respect all students. Treat gang members like students and not as behavior problems. Above all, have high expectations for academic achievement. Talk only to individual students, one-on-one about gang involvement and not in front of the class.

2. Set definite rules for all students and enforce them equally for everyone and for all unacceptable behavior. If need be suspend, and file charges, if needed. Gang kids respect and expect a discipline structure.

3. Keep current on gang culture, dress, etc.

4. Give gang member's responsibility that enhances their self-esteem, such as assigning them as tutors, and helpers.

5. Show concern and compassion for all students as well as for gang members.

6. Remember that their culture may dictate that they maintain a humble demeanor

7. Provide multi-cultural and a rigorous academic curriculum

Don'ts

1. Don't publicly praise a gang member for academic achievement or other achievement before asking the student if it is ok to praise them.

2. Don't talk about gangs, gang activity or incidents with your class or group of students

3. Don't change your mind about your rules-do not make exceptions. Gang kids see inconsistencies as a weakness and exploit it.

4. Don't trust them completely.

5. Don't become a homie to gang kids

6. Don't make promises to help or threaten action for misdeeds and then not follow through.

7. Don't patronize minorities by only addressing their culture during culture weeks, such as: Martin Luther King's birthday, cinco de mayo, etc. Remember, they exist every day in your classroom.

FOCUSING ON THE GANGS IN SCHOOL:

1. Most gang-affiliated youth are not alienated from the school objectives of education, only with the delivery of the objectives and education.

2. Administration tactics that focus attention on a gang raise the gang's prestige on campus.

3. This chapter recommends a five-fold approach:

a. The gang phenomenon at school should be downplayed so that it becomes less relevant to members, other pupils, and educators. They should be de-emphasized and ignored except when essential to school order.

b. The structural looseness of gangs and the value most members place on education provide educators the opportunity to concentrate more on the education and socialization of individual members and less on their control. However, don't try to control behaviors that are not specifically forbidden.

c. Orient teachers about gang youth. They must be made to realize that the gang is only one aspect of a member's life, and recognize gang members for their individual qualities. This includes a disregard for harmless gang customs and Idiosyncratic behaviors.

d. Tolerance of the appearance and mannerisms of gang members will reduce a major source of friction and will protect unaffiliated students whose cholo dress elicits inaccurate labeling. To notice the baseball caps whether worn backwards, sideways, or any other ways reflects all the energy, enthusiasm, optimism, craziness, fun, or the vibrancy of life of students.

James Kauffman (1994) stated, "We are in no danger of becoming a nation of wimps; we are in imminent danger of becoming a nation of thugs. We know the details of violence among children and youth in our society. We recite the litany of this violence with shame, sorrow, disgust, and terror. However, for decades we have failed to act on what we know about the causes of violence and aggression. We can't afford to delay effective action any longer."

MINIMIZING GANG INVOLVEMENT ACTIVITIES

1.Opportunities Provision:

In high school special focus should be on improved education, employment training, and job placement are needed if they want the gang situation to improve. Improved education is available in most school districts, but the schools need to focus on the education and objectives of gang members. Employment training and placement need to be realistic. When a kid can make hundred of dollars selling drugs, can we really expect them to give up selling drugs to work at McDonalds?

Unfortunately, there aren't many good paying jobs in the rural areas. Consequently, part of their training needs to focus on legal and illegal behaviors and convince them to be law-abiding citizens while working in low paying jobs.

2.Social Intervention:

The focus should be on the individual behavior and value change. This dovetails into the suggestions mentioned on 1 above.

3.Community mobilization:

Grassroots participation and inter-agency networking are essential. Law enforcement, and the schools can't do it alone. The total community has to be involved when addressing this issue. We can no longer wait, or criticize the schools and the police. The community's motto ought to be, "If we are not part of the solution; we are part of the problem."

4. Organizational and development Strategies:

Specialized units such as a police gang unit, Probation unit, police officers housed in schools as is normally done in Merced County in California. The District Attorney's gang unit should all work as a team. This does not mean that the rest of the community can sit back and hope for the best. However, all the personal involved need to do the right things and not continue doing the wrong things to suppress gang activity. These agencies either work together, or the gangs will win.

5. Suppression and Incarceration:

Arrest and incarceration should be the final act because these actions reinforce gang membership, but only after every thing possible has been attempted or accomplished by the total community. None of the factors mentioned here precludes the teachers because teachers get to know and understand the students and they can be the first line of defense, but the rest of the community needs to be supportive and aid the classroom teacher.

TO MINIMIZE GANGS AND VIOLENCE, THE SCHOOLS OF THE FUTURE MUST SERVE MANY NEEDS:

1. Teachers should not instruct so much and instead be guides to students in the learning process where multiculturalism thrives, where students can walk down the hall to talk to a counselor about their parent's divorce, physical abuse, alcohol or drug abuse, and confidentiality is crucial. Beginning teachers can only teach one thing effectively to students and that is for them to "learn." Once they learn to learn then the students can learn other curriculum subjects.

2. The schools of the future can no longer be the "tribal centers" of the past that promoted Protestant morality and community pride, or were just learning factories, or hospitals to redress social ills, and where students with limited learning abilities did not attend school. Those days are gone and school districts need to join the 21st. century.

3. The new schools must be: (1) multicultural centers, and (2) knowledge-learner centers.

a. For schools to become multicultural centers there must be: continued attention to cultural bias and sensitivity. Appreciation and promotion of diversity in the profession, as well as in assessments and intervention of all students should be the emphasis.

b. Advocate for the promotion of tolerance and appreciation of cultural diversity in the schools, and against discriminatory school practices. However, school psychologists and counselors can't do it all because there is a shortage of both in these positions and as budgets become less and less these are the people that are the first to go.

c. For schools to change from "factories" to knowledge-based education the curriculum must change as well as the school structure, where teachers become information guides rather than instructors and, School psychologists must become more involved in developing prevention programs.

d. Advocate for reorganization of schools away from assessing students towards nurturing and supporting them and instead educate them. This may be an impossibility because the current trend, in schools, is to prepare students to pass a standardized test rather than teaching students to learn the academic subjects.

e. Schools should be full-service health centers, as proposed by a former US Surgeon General and some key legislators who advocate for school-based or school-linked health clinics for the students. However, too often school boards are busy balancing budgets and other functions related to board businesses, which may not be related to the benefits of the teachers and students.

Consequently, they don't think they have time to address the gang issue and would prefer to just send them to juvenile hall. Unfortunately, far too many students are gang members, or school shooters as it was at Columbine school in Colorado. If school boards do not focus on gangs and school violence then Dr. Kauffman could be right when he stated that we may be producing a "nation of thugs!"

It is also understood, by the author, that federal and state mandates, to improve test scores for future funding places teachers in the position of teaching to the test, or simply teaching the test. All of this in the name of "accountability."

Will the students learn under these mandates? Who knows, some students will learn, but they will be the exception. The federal and state governments need to remove themselves from the education business and let the teachers do their job. If they don't, who knows what will happen to the future American youth. To reiterate, the teachers are the first line of defense and teachers must be provided with all the resources possible, by the administrators, the school board, and to teach the students fairly and equally so that gang membership is minimized. But we must remember that the total community must be totally involved in the prevention of gangs.

CLOSURE FOR THIS CHAPTER

The teachers and school administrators have been the focus of this chapter and it is hoped that "others" don't expect that educating is a process of prevention of gangs and school violence. It must be remembered that students are in school six hours per day and the rest of the time they are home or walking the streets causing destruction or killing each other. Neither of these factors should be an option for young people.

As yet there is still not an overall community effort to address the gang problem. Yes, there have been many efforts to form committees to combat this issue, but usually some of the most important people are not included. Or the people themselves may not want to or refuse to get involved. While top school administrators are sometimes included we fail to remember that many of them have not been in the classroom since the gang issues became a problem. Hence, the teacher's involvement is crucial!

CHAPTER FOUR

THE ROLE OF PARENTS IN THE PREVENTION OF GANGS IN THE CLASSROOM

This chapter is written for the parents to: increase their awareness and understanding of the nature and challenge of gangs, to Identify signs and signals of pre-gang (wanna bee's) involvement, to identify resources for prevention and intervention, and to identify the motives for gang involvement of their children.

Parents ought to know that gangs exist in all cities and towns. Some of the ethnic groups who are involved in gangs are African American (Black) Mexican/ Latino, and Southeast Asians such as the Lao, Hmong, Mien, Cambodians, and Vietnamese. Picking out gang members is not much of a problem if parents just look at the clothes they wear, especially if the clothes have the colors red and blue, as well as hand signals, tattoos, and even the way they walk. Parents must also know who their friends are and what are their new hobbies.

However, many parents often do not want to admit that their children, who are also students, are involved in gang activity because parents believe it makes them look bad, or they simply may not want to admit their children's gang participation.

One of the first things parents need to understand is that their view of the world is different from a youth's view of the world. The adult's view of the youth culture is often different from the actual youth's culture. However, the youth's point of view of the world may not be understood by many adults, for example skateboarding, Many cities now have skate parks, but the youth still skate where it is not allowed. For the youth skating becomes a challenge and parks do not present a challenge, therefore, they skate where it is forbidden. Meanwhile, the adults are bewildered because the skaters don't use the parks to do all their skating.

Consequently, adults are amazed that what they dictate is often not adhered to by the youth. As parents we ought to have youthful mindsets that relate to youth. This requires that the parents recognize their youngsters" new trends, style in clothing, what do the kids see as "hip" and what is not so that they know if the kids are going through new trends, or seem interested in joining a gang. Hence, they must think like the youth, as some of us did, Let us remember that when Elvis first came into the entertainment scene, the adults hated his music, singing, and body gyrations. But the teenagers loved him. When did the teenagers cease to like Elvis? When the adults accepted him and learned to like his music and singing and his gyrations no longer bothered the adults. The reason for this example is to show parents that if they don't like RAP or other teenage music, all they have to do is pretend that they, the adults, like it then the teenagers will find other music to listen to, and the process begins again.

In some cases it may be fortunate that they normally have large families and the children may not have individual, or private bedrooms. Therefore, in many minority cultures the parents do visit their children's bedroom and are able to detect gang activity. However, parents must learn how to detect gang activity by their kids. New immigrants may view their children as they did in the old country and have not learned that they do not have total control over their children, and may be totally unaware of gang activities and gang memberships in the USA. The parents must realize that their youngsters may be losing their culture and language and do so by choice because they want to escape from the "old" culture. Belonging to a gang may be one way to escape from the old culture and language.

Moreover, the parents may use "punishment" that is contrary to the American child abuse laws. "For instance, many Latino parents may come from a country where the teacher is allowed to discipline or punish the children and they do not comprehend the message when the teacher complains to the parent's about their child's behavior. The idea in the minds of the parents may be "why tell me about it, you are the teacher and have total control so take care of the child's behavior."

Parents have to understand that the laws of the new country related to discipline are very different from the old country and teachers are forbidden to "punish" students. Consequently, parents will lose control of their children because no one is disciplining the youngster and becoming a gang member before the parents learn about gangs in this country.

However, the new immigrants are not alone because many American parents and agencies are as unaware of gang activity as are the new immigrants. This chapter was written to aide parents in identifying the early warning signs of street gang activities and how they impact their children and the family structure.

Parents also need to know where their youngsters are, whom they are with, and what they are doing when they are not at home because gang violence is increasing. This will prevent the parents from receiving a phone call, in the middle of the night, telling them that their son, or daughter, has killed someone, or worse yet, that one of their kids has been shoot and killed. This can be a parent's worse nightmare, but gang violence happens every day. Consequently, parents need to know and understand more about gangs in the schools and community. This is often a difficult task because some parents work long hours in minimum paying jobs and they may feel that they don't have time to learn about gangs.

Consequently, the author's message to parents is to be good role models and to establish standards for acceptable behavior in the home, at school, and enforced for violation of these standards. If parents are dishonest, abuse drugs and/or alcohol, if they are violent and lack respect for others, they can be sure that their children will probably exhibit the same behavior they have observed at home. If parents are not good role models, or think that they are not, an inventory of their life style to find out why your child is a potential or already a gang member.

Above all learn about gangs because kids as young as 9 or 10 are wanna bee's or have already joined a gang. It may not make sense to parents, but it does to their child. Many gang members say that they joined a gang because the gang offered them support, caring, a sense of safety, order and purpose. These are the things that parents are supposed to be providing and they must provide them. If parents do this, the odds of their child not joining a gang is very good because then their children will see no value in gang membership.

What is a gang? A gang is a group of people that hang around or associate, on a regular basis, in a negative way, they are involved in criminal activities, or have a common name and symbols. If they dress alike wearing certain type of clothing, fight with other groups, or act violently toward others and many have nicknames that other hommies use toward them. These factors indicate gang involvement. Many claim an area, such as their bedroom, as their territory, and project arrogance, and display a defiant attitude. Who can join a gang? Anyone!

SOME REASONS WHY YOUNGSTERS JOIN GANGS

1. Stress. Do children have stress? Certainly! It effects them in at least three ways: physical, emotionally, and behavioral. When children become overburdened with stress they are likely to feel "out of control" which leads to anger and can be vented through "gang involvement."

2. A sense of belonging to a family. The need to be loved, accepted, and protected by one's family and siblings is essential to the child's healthy self-concept. If these needs are not met at home then they will join a gang to belong to a family.

3. Peer Pressure by influential individuals, or hero-types, want youngsters to join a gang and children do not want to be seen as nerds, eggheads, or too bookish.

4. Excitement. The need for adventure and being involved in daring "risky behavior" is a strong motivation.

5. Gangs provide protection. If they need for group or peer support to resist assaults or attacks from other people or gangs are not met, the kids will join a gang.

6. Low Self esteem. Children become attracted to and involved in negative destructive behavior when they do not like themselves and develop an "I don't care attitude."

7. Substance abuse

8. Physical and or sexual abuse

9. To earn money

10 Recreation, girls, or boys and drugs

11. Resist living like their parents

12. Protection from others

13. Recognition and self-esteem

14. Family member already in a gang

Parents need to be aware of these factors if they want to keep their children from joining gangs. It is very difficult to accomplish all that has been said because many parents live a busy life. However, if parents don't make time to help their children then the worse may happen to their children. The bottom line is that if their children are already wanna bees, or gang members the parents my have already lost their children to the gangs. But, if they love their children enough, it is never too late to keep trying to save them. How can a parent know or suspect that their children may be a wanna bee or gang member? The following may be of some help.

RISK FACTORS THAT COULD AFFECT SOCIETY

- Presence of gang members in household
- Poor school achievement and poor relationships with teachers and parents
- Deviant youth contacts by the youngster
- Presence of or using drugs

TYPES OF GANGS THAT CHILDREN MAY BE INVOLVED IN

1. There are street gangs with an emphasis on location and or geographic boundaries. They usually claim their territory in cities/town, or neighborhood with graffiti, street names, or area codes.

2. There are posses or crews. There may be small groups who are used for specific purposes, such as committing crime or dealing in drugs.

3. There are wanna bee's; they are the "pretend" gangs and are usually the youth may imitate older gang members

4. There are criminal organizations, they are disciplined and are structured groups who commit serious crimes for profit or other motives such as killing rival gang members. These are definitely the hard-core members.

5. Parents can also look for certain markings around the home, lunch boxes, back packs, or body tattoos. Some of these markings are known as graffiti and below are some examples of graffiti they may find.

Common Graffiti that parents can identify or if they see any of the following

C.R.I.P.S.   MOD   XIV   XIII   W/S = Westside, E/S = Eastside, S/S
Southside N/S = North side.
The Bloods and the Latin gang members also use these designations.

BLOODS	LB	OB
Sur	LF	XIII-or 3- or "eme"
NORTE	BDG	F-14
ESF	14NIPS	X3
F-13	NVP	209
107	TRG	KMD

Any of these graffiti signs indicate that youngsters are wanna bee's or gang members. Please refer to the chapter related to graffiti.

As has been stated repeatedly, there are gangs all over the United States, in every state, town, or city. Even in small agricultural towns of 900 population. In this chapter the author concentrates on the San Joaquin Valley, in central California because the author lives in this part of California. However, much of his information applies to other localities in every sate of the nation. In this 21st century there are at least 71 gangs in one county surrounding Merced County California, and many other gangs in the other counties of the San Joaquin Valley. Some of the Mexican gangs may use the word "CHICALI". This term originated in the Imperial Valley of California. "Chi" stands for Chicano and CALI is short for Mexicali Mexico. Parents need to understand that the average age of gang members are 8-35 years of age.

Consequently, parents should not believe that their children are too young to join gangs because they are not and the lower age is getting younger and younger. In Fresno California, there are about 600 active gang members who commit crimes daily. The Asian gangs are very mobile, but usually they don't declare a territory. They often imitate signs and language of African American, or Latino gangs. However, the terms or words may be used in the native language. The Asian gangs often prey on their own people because they know that Asians keep valuables in the home because the elders do not trust banks.

The Fresno/Clovis (California) police use the following guidelines for identifying gang members and it is very useful for parents for possible gang identification. These include:

1. Having gang tattoos. Note many Asians do not use the degrading tattoos on their bodies.
2. Wearing gang clothing that includes the color (blue or red) of clothing, head covering, or methods of grooming for particular gangs.
3, Kids displaying gang markings or slogans on personal property or clothing.
4. How they button the top buttons of their shirt, it can be 3 or 4 buttons, buttoned which signifies 13 And 14.
5. Admitting to gang membership.
6. Anyone being arrested with known gang members or youngsters attending functions sponsored by the gang or known gang members, parents obtaining information from reliable informants, or parents getting information from relatives identifying the youth as a gang member.
7. Parents or police receiving information from other law enforcement agencies that a youth is a gang member from various sources, such as being stopped by police with a known gang member.
8. Loitering, riding, or meeting with gang members. If youngsters are selling or distributing drugs for a known gang member and helping known gang member commit a crime.

It only takes exhibiting one of these characteristics for a youth to be considered a gang member or wanna bee. Two of these can result in a youth being labeled an associate gang member. Displaying five or more of these characteristics can cause police to identify someone as a hard-core gang member. The current law also uses gang membership to extend the sentencing of gang members. This means that if a gang member is sentenced to five years in prison for a given crime, the judge can add more years to the sentence because they are certified gang members..

GANG CLOTHING

There are good visuals on clothing that is very important to gang members. This information can further help the parents to identify or suspect their children to be wanna bees or gang members. The "gang look" is meant to intimidate those kids who are not in a gang. The kids who dress in clothing that resembles gang clothing or are showing an interest in gangs, they attract the attention of gangs, and could be putting themselves in danger

In recent years youngsters, who were not gang members, have been shot or killed by gang members who thought the youngsters were gang rivals just because they wore gang related clothing of a different color. Consequently, many kids are hurt or killed for wearing the wrong color clothing, however, they were innocent, and were not gang members. For the safety of your own youngsters, it is important that you do not buy or allow your kids to wear any item that gang members use to identify with a gang, such as clothing with the colors "black, red and blue." Also look for the following style of clothing:

1. White oversized T shirts and creased in the back right down the middle
2. White athletic type undershirt.
3. Black, gray, or brown oversized Dickey or Khaki beige work pants.
4. The pants worn are low or sagging and cuffed inside at the bottom or dragging on the ground.
5. Baseball caps worn backwards or sideways, and usually black or
sometimes with the initials of the gang. For instance, the Hispanic gang members may wear a cap with the initials NY (for New York), because it can mean "Norteño Youth."
6. Hairnets.
7. They often wear dark or dull clothing of one particular color
8. Black football or basketball clothing. This is changing and now gang
members can any color that can mean anything when wearing any NFL jacket.
For instance, any color NFL jacket can be worn and NFL can mean Nuestra Familia Lives or Loca, Our Crazy Family or Our Family lives.
9. Pin striped imitation baseball type oversized shirt.
10. All white tennis shoes with black shoelaces, all black shoes with white shoelaces, or the shoelaces may be the color of a gang.
11. Black woven crosses worn around the neck used by Latino. The prisoners make these crosses.

Note: the gang related clothing for girls is similar to those worn by the boys. However, please read the chapter that describes clothing and baseball caps for more understanding of these subjects.

PARENTS NEED TO UNDERSTAND THAT DISCIPLINE WORKS BETTER THAN PUNISHMENT

Discipline means guidance, it stands for rules and standards we use to live our lives. Discipline does not mean punishment, such as spankings, or other physical violence. Discipline is used to help children develop self-control. Discipline is setting limits and correcting negative behaviors. It is used for encouraging children, and guiding them, helping them feel good about themselves, and teach them how to think for themselves. It is an important part of life, and plays a part in everything people do. From manners we learn, at home, the limits that are set and enforced by the laws of the home and the community.

Punishment means some type of physical violence, such as whipping and this includes spanking, slapping and paddling. However, some parents may feel that slapping, spanking, and paddling is not punishment because it is not "whipping." If parents use punishment, it should be used only in extreme cases and using the bare hands only. If punishment is administered, and the author advises, against it, it should be for discipline, or correction and immediate after the offense. Consequently, it should be administered immediately and related to the act and of short duration. If punishment is administered for very long, the child may become resentful and act out to seek revenge. Remember that violence breed's violence by the one giving and the one receiving it. Be careful when punishment is administered and punishment should only be used in very extreme cases. For better understanding between discipline and punishment, the following is listed:

Discipline	Punishment
1. Is used to teach.	1. Is used to hurt, cause pain and teaches violence.
2. Used as positive communication.	2. It is communication of displeasure or none acceptance.
3. It helps the child develop inner-control.	3. Child relies on out side control
4. Creates a sense of self-worth and high self esteem.	4. Creates a feeling of low self esteem and little pride.

5. Helps children grow.	5. Can lead to anti-social behavior and violence.
6. It is often taught by example.	6. Is taught by negative example.

PARENTS CAN LOOK FOR OTHER SIGNS IF THEY SUSPECT THEIR CHILDREN MAY BE A GANG MEMBER OR WANT S TO BE ONE:

1. School attendance problems and grades drop at school.

2. Changing of clothing style such as baggy pants and overly large sized shirts.

3. They start getting tattoos painted on them.

4. There are signs of graffiti in their room, on their books, clothes, and other belongings.

5. Look for a change of attitude, mood swings, losing respect for the parent and using a different language at home, sometimes it is foul.

6. May have severe cigarette burns that may come from gang initiation.

7. Starting to smoke legal or illegal cigarettes.

8. May run away from home.

PARENTS CAN MINIMIZE REASONS YOUNGSTERS FROM JOINING GANGS.

Parents can begin by entering their youngster's room to see if there are any signs of gang writings, clothing with the colors red or blue. Or anything that may look different from the usual items parents buys their youngsters. However, the most important thing a parent can do is to meet their youngster's friends with the following in mind: Who are they? How much influence do they have on my kids? How do they spend their free time? If your youngster has friends that are gang members, then they are probably involved or will become involved in a gang.

Parent must remember that their youngsters may be looking for a loving family relationship and if parents don't provide one, the gangs will.

Consequently, have good and positive communication with your children. This allows your youngsters to come to you to discuss any topic, concern, or problem. Good communication allows <u>parents to tell their youngsters that they are loved</u>. However, do not buy or allow your youngsters to dress in what you suspect may be some type of gang clothing. Do not allow your youngsters to stay out late, or spend a lot of unsupervised time out in the streets. Teach them respect for other people's property, and don't allow them to write any gang symbols on any of their belongings, including their room.

Above all, learn about gang and drug activities in your community. Learn how gang members, dress, speak, and how they behave. Become involved and become an informed parent. There are many meetings and workshops in the community for you to attend. However, parents must have a deep desire to keep their youngsters from joining gangs, even if it means missing their favorite TV program, or other personal desires. And remember the education and welfare of parent's children is much too important to leave to teachers to teach them everything. But teachers do take care of your youngster's educational needs, and indeed they may keep your children from danger or death, but parents must remember that they are their youngster's first teacher. Parent s must take responsibility to be an integral part of their child's education. Remember that the schools and teachers have your child for only 6 hours a day and it is up to the parent to make positive use of the other 18 hours of their child's life. Parents can make education fruitful and to be part of their youngster's education.

Above all parents should not make excuses or become an enabler to their youngsters. For example, A few years ago a mother who's son was a drug addict and when others ask about the son, the mother would say that the son was ill and in bed. The son was doped up and would not work or socialize with his friends because he was under the influence of drugs. One day she went into the son's bedroom to tell him to eat something. Her son did not move because he had over dosed on heroin and was dead. One can say that this mother loved her son to death. Unfortunately there are many more mothers that are doing the same thing and one of these days their son will also be found dead from an over dose.

The message for mothers is, "do not love your youngsters to death!"

CHAPTER 5

COMPARING SCHOOL SHOOTINGS
AND GANG VIOLENCE

Neither school nor gang violence should be tolerated because both lead to the death of the youth/Gang violence includes many innocent victims, but in the case of school violence all the victims have been innocent/Consequently, this chapter compares the two types of violence in order to provide some knowledge to the schools, parents and society. Hopefully society and the schools can glean some information from this book in order to formulate violence prevention programs. Some of these programs are included in other chapters. Conversely, one big difference between the two-types of violence is that school violence is being conducted by suburban middle class White youth. Accordingly, society cannot place the blame on this type violence on inner-city youth. The author also hopes that the universities take active roles in teaching about these two problems to student teachers, or the newly credentialed teachers who will need this knowledge. The new to be or teachers need to learn about the real world before they begin teaching in public schools. They also need to understand the social problems they will encounter in the real world of teaching where there are gang members and school shooters in the K-12 classrooms. This is a reality that the new teachers will face and they are not being provided the knowledge or tools to address the problem of gang memberships and school violence.

To emphasize this phenomenon the following article is included.

The Modesto Bee (located in Modesto California) Newspaper Reported:

One question we don't ask about the rash of school shootings is, "Why are they happening in mostly white and suburban schools?" Why aren't they happening in inner-city schools? There is no question that school violence is just as pervasive, if not more so, in the "hood" as in the"burbs," but there is a different social matrix in the inner city. Lets begin by calling these school shootings exactly what they are: SUICIDES. With the exception of the two boys in Jonesboro, Ark., there was no attempt or even intent to escape. They either killed themselves, (Columbine), expected to be killed, but they did not surrender to face life imprisonment, or eventual execution.

These suicides were accompanied by the desire to kill as many others as possible on their way out of this world. This pattern of suicide could be called "the Samson syndrome" at the end of the biblical story of Samson, we find him betrayed and weakened; his eyes gouged out and subjected to humiliation for the entertainment off the Philistines. As he stands between the pillars of the temple, in one final, desperate act, he pulls the pillars down, killing himself and 3,000 Philistines.

For the boys in today's school shootings, the bullies, the athletes, and the homecoming queen, or the "Big Man" on campus are all pillars of the school temple that they must destroy. In one final desperate act, they are destroying as many "Philistines" as they can. But what else can we say about the children who commit these acts? Can we identify them in advance?

Psychologist Bryan Nichols, who works with the LA. Bridges gang diversion program says,

In almost every case the perpetrator is a child who has suffered a significant narcissistic injury. That is their sense of self, already fragile due to weakness born of physical frailty, biological limitations and or parental inattention, becomes annihilated by assault from an outside agency such as the bully, a girl friend, parent or other enemy. They then feel compelled to end their lives with the satisfaction of an inordinate and overwhelming display of power. (Page B7)

To return to the mystery of why these events happen in suburban, rural and city schools. The author can only say that so far school violence is not taking place in inner city schools. Consequently, there must be an examination of the school matrix of the inner city schools to obtain statistics that will help in this crisis and to change the negative behaviors to become positive behaviors. The same psychological problems exist in inner cities, but there are different outlets there that can help suburbia. In the inner city, some weak and bullied kids find protection and a degree of acceptance in a gang. In the case of the Latino gangs these kids are recruited because they are vulnerable and they are offered a pseudo family within the gang structure. Being a member of a gang allows them to insulate themselves from the raw and seemingly relentless assaults on their ego that they would otherwise have to endure. As gang members, they are vicariously empowered by the fearful respect given to the group. Even the bullies are at bay because, in the inner city, the bullies are more typically the gang leaders who are the strong disciplinarians and who mete out punishment for those gang members that deserve punishment. The schools can be very effective in turning negative behaviors into positive ones and perhaps both gangs and school shootings would decrease to a manageable crisis.

The violence of the gang is often random, but it is not suicidal. Gang members always plan to get away. Which explains the drive-by shootings. They may spray the front of a school or a house in a rival's territory, but they don't stay long enough for the body count to climb into the dozens. Neither have they engaged the technology of the bomb. Another reason the Samson syndrome doesn't happen in the inner city is because youngsters that have the most potential for violence are in gangs. This allows the community to respond with gang diversion and prevention programs.

However, in the suburban (the burbs) settings these damaged kids add isolation to their predicament. While acting in tandem at times, this arrangement does not rise to the level of a gang. They are basically loners who live on the fringes of their culture. With noses pressed up against the glass of the hatred mainstream society. They live isolated lives, even in their own homes, where parents often do not even bother to enter their rooms. But by entering their parental rooms, many of these children find the weapons they need for their deadly acts.

Until we admit that these events, wherever they happen, are a product of our over all culture and our social condition and not unpredictable acts of sociopathic kids, they will continue to happen. These kids will walk by our sides, sit in our classrooms and live in our shadows. Then, in one final act of desperation, they will take the temple down, leaving us only with our now pathetic refrain: "I never thought it could happen here."

School violence is occurring in many states and schools. Some states are passing laws against school violence and or bulling. But the violence continues because we still have not gotten the message about the youth culture. We still don't seem to know what we can do about it. More importantly is the fact that we don't believe it will happen in our community. This "head in the sand" attitude will not help combat a very dangerous condition. Quite often it is the adults that set the example for the youngsters. Many adults are competitive to a dangerous fault. We have heard of some fathers killing other fathers over a kid's athletic game. Let us ask our selves, "is learning good sportsmanship by the youth who play soccer, football, basketball, and baseball the goal of sports?"

A short visit to any of these games on a Saturday morning, one can see some of these games, played by children, and you will also see that these sports are often for the benefit of the parents who are supposed to set the example. However, parents often cuss out the officials, and even their own kids if they make a mistake because all the parents want - is to win. Our favorite saying is: "it is not whether we win or lose, but how we play the game!" This is normally said when a team loses a game. However, the next thing the coach says is, "next week you better not lose." Lets face it, as Americans we hate to lose and what message do we send to our Children? Is it any wonder why we create violent children?

RECENT (as of 2005) EXAMPLES OF SCHOOL VIOLENCE

Bethel Regional High School in Bethel, Alaska

Evan Ramsey was an outcast, a status earned by his slight frame, shy manner, poor grades, and broken family. He said, "I got stuff thrown at me, I got spit on, I got beat up. Sometimes I fought back, but I wasn't that good at fighting." Taunted throughout his years in school, he reported the incidents to his teachers, and at first his tormentors were punished. "After a while the principal told me to just start ignoring everybody. But then I couldn't take it anymore." On Feb. 19, 1997 Ramsey, then 16, went to school with a 12-guage shotgun... killing a 16-year-old basketball star and the 50-year-old principal. He was tried as an adult for murder and was sentenced to 210 years in prison. In prison Ramsey admits in his cell, in Seward Alaska, "I felt power with a gun. It was the only way to get rid of my anger."

Columbine High School in Colorado

Unfortunately, Ramsey is not alone. Children all over the country are feeling fear, hopelessness, and rage, emotions that turn some students into bullies, and others into victims. At a time when many parents are afraid to send their children to school, the wake-up call sounded by the 13 killings and 2 suicides at Columbine High School in Colorado not very long ago and it still reverberates. It is now clear that Dylan Klebold and Eric Harris felt bullied and alienated, and in their minds it was "payback time." However, the question often asked is, "how could these kids have an arsenal of weapons in their bedroom and the parents didn't know anything about it?"

Santana High School in Santee, California

On March 15, 2001 Charles Andy Williams brought a .22-cal. pistol to Santana High School in Santee. California and shot 15 students and adults, killing two people. What was his apparent motive? Lethal revenge for the torment he had known at the hands of local kids. "We abused him pretty much, I mean verbally, concedes one of them. " called him a skinny faggot one time. In June 2002 he plead guilty and was sent to prison.

Williamsport, Pennsylvania

Two days after the Williams shooting, Elizabeth Bush, 14, and an eighth grader from Williamsport, Pa., who said she was often called an "idiot, stupid, fat and ugly," brought her father's .22 cal. pistol and shot 13-year-old Kimberly Marchese, wounding her in the shoulder. Kimberly, one of her few friends, had earned Elizabeth's ire by allegedly turning on her and lining in with the taunters. Elizabeth is now a ward of the court until she turns 21; she is now in a juvenile psychiatric facility.

Etowah High School, Atlanta, Georgia

Although this is not a typical school violence example, one of the most shocking cases of victimization by bullies took place near Atlanta on March 28, 1994. On that day, 15-year old Brian Head, a heavyset sophomore at suburban Etowah High School, walked into his economics class, pulled out his father's 9-mm handgun and pressed it to his temple. I can't take this anymore," he said. Then he squeezed the trigger. Brian had been teased for years about his weight. A lot of times the more popular or athletic kids would make him a target. His mother Rita says of her only child, "They would slap Brian in the back of the head or push him into a locker. Until finally it just broke him."

Powell High School in Powell, Tennessee

Josh Sneed may never forgive the boys he refers to as the skaters. It was in 1996 late in his freshman year at Powell High School in Powell, Tenn., when he says a group of skateboarders began to terrorize him... they chased him and threatened to beat him to death. Why Josh? He was small and a "country boy." Says his mother. "They made fun of him for that. They told him he was poor and made fun of him for that." Then on Oct. 17, 1996, "I just snapped," her son says. As Jason Pratt, known as one of the skaters, passed him in the cafeteria, Sneed whacked him on the head with a tray. "I figured that if I got lucky and took him out, all the other nonsense would stop." But after a few punches, Josh slipped on a scrap of food, hit his head on the floor and lost consciousness as Pratt kneed him in the head several times. Finally a football player saved his life. Josh was badly hurt and suffered a shattered skull. He had to relearn how to walk and talk. Home schooled Josh finally earned his GED, but he hasn't regained his short-term memory. Assault charges against both him and Pratt were dismissed, but Pratt was suspended from school for 133 days. Josh now says, "Everybody's hollering that they need to get rid of guns, but it is not just that, he says, "You need to find out what is going on in school."

School violence is a serious problem in our schools today, as the examples listed above, relating to the violence occurring in various school sites have shown. It is the responsibility of all educators to be able to recognize the warning sings of possible violence and to intervene appropriately. The following are warning signs, or ideas identified by the American Psychological Association.

The concept of power, or what is meant by power

48 As school enrollment rises and youths cope with the mounting pressures of today's competitive and status-conscious culture, the numbers of bullied children have grown rapidly as a consequences. A lot of kids have grief, loss, pain, and it seems to remain unresolved. Some experts see bulling as an inevitable consequence of a culture that rewards perceived strength and dominance. "The concept of power 49 we admire is power over someone else," says Jackson Katz, 41, whose Long Beach, Calif., consulting firm counsels schools and the military on violence prevention.

In the corporate culture, in sports culture and in the media, we honor those who win at all costs. The bully is a kind of hero in our society. A Secret Service study in the fall of 2000, found that in two-thirds of the 37 school shootings since 1974, the attackers felt "persecuted, bullied, threatened, attacked, or injured." In more than three-quarters of the cases, the attacker told a peer of his violent intentions. Several boys from Columbine described bulling as part of the school fabric. Two admitted to mocking Klebold and Harris. "Why don't people get it that it drives you over the edge? It isn't just Columbine. It is everywhere."

Society needs to show or teach youngsters how to address their emotional and physical abuses that in too many cases leads to gang membership, or student violence. To accomplish this a school psychologist, or social worker needs to be assigned in every K-5 school. Or at the very least there ought to be an adult that the students can go to for addressing the students abuse and bullying.

The following signs occurring over a period of time may increase the potential for school violence:

1. A history of violence or aggressive behavior that can be either verbal or physical behavior
2. Serious drug or alcohol use.
3. Gang membership or desire to be in a gang.
4. Fascination with weapons, especially guns.
5. Threatening others regularly.
6. Trouble controlling anger.
7. Withdrawal from friends and usual activities.
8. Feeling rejected or alone.
9. Having been a victim of bullying.
10. Poor school performance.
11. History of discipline problems.
12. Feeling constantly disrespected.
13. Failing to acknowledge the feeling or rights of others.

Immediate warning signs that violence is a serious possibility in schools

1. Loss of temper on a daily basis.
2. Frequent physical fighting.
3. Significant vandalism or property damage.
4. Increase in use of drugs or alcohol.
5. Increase in risk-taking behavior.
6. Detailed plans to commit acts of violence.
7. Announcing threats or plans for hurting others.
8. Enjoying hurting animals.
9. Carrying a weapon.

Factors that contribute to violent behavior

1. Peer pressure.
2. Need for attention or respect.
3. Feeling of low self-worth.
4. Early childhood abuse or neglect.
5. Witnessing violence at home, in the community, or in the media.
6. Easy access to weapons.
7. Being bullyed.

Much of the problem in school violence is due to bullying. If society heeds what the individual's involvement in school violence the key factor are that there are students who were bullied by other "more powerful" students, consequently, the issues of bullying need to be addressed.

BULLYS AND BULLYING

Schools and parents ought to be knowledgeable about "bulling in the schools." Society can no longer be in denial that bulling doesn't exist, is not relevant, or is harmless, in the schools. School shootings are serious and we need to act before there are more of them. Bullies need to be disciplined consistently and immediately.

Bullying is defined as, "aggressive behaviors by one person or group carried out repeatedly and over time and targeted at someone less powerful." Siobhan McDonough, Modesto Bee, states, to fight Crime: Invest in Kids, says a national advocacy group. The report came from a news conference in Washington D. C. The report stated, "Still not much has been done to prevent bullying in US schools." The report also states," ... that for children in grades 6 through 10 nearly 3.2 million are victims of bullying. The report citing US and European studies states: "Programs to prevent bullying are relatively inexpensive It costs very little for large school districts to establish funds to create safe and drug free schools.

How can parents tell when their child is being bullied--- or bullying others? The author suggests that the following also apply to teachers and administrators. In 1993... The Cherry Creek School District in Englewood Colo. published Bully-proofing your school. One of its co-authors Dr. William Porter, a clinical psychologist, offers the following guidelines for parents.

Dealing with bullies:

A bully is a child who takes repeated hostile actions against another child and has more power than the individual he targets. Bullies tend to be very glib and can't accept responsibility for their behavior.

How do I know if my child is being bullied?

The youngsters may show an unwillingness to go to school and may have bruises on their body, or damage to their belongings that can't be explained. Children who are being bullied tend to keep silent about it and may become withdrawn, depressed and feel no one can help.

What can I do if my child is being bullied?

Parents and teachers must listen to the child and express confidence that the problem can be solved. Keep trying until you find someone at school to help. Practice with your child such protective skills as avoiding the confrontation or using humor to deflate a tense moment.

What if my child is a bully?

Set clear and consistent expectations of behavior, and work with the school on follow-up. Don't let the child talk his or her way out of the behavior, and find positives for him or her to get their attention.

BULLYING PREVENTION

In the last few years, incidents of violent retributions have led to an increase awareness of the problem of bulling. It has existed for years, but it has often been overlooked in the schools. Yet bulling has detrimental psychological effects on students, such as a negative self-esteem, depression, and often suicide. Much of the bulling is done in school. In the United States, approximately 20 % of students are bullied (Whitney & Smith 1993). Most bullying occurs, with very little adult supervision in places such as playgrounds and hallways. The victims are usually less popular, and often without a single friend in school, they tend to be more anxious and insecure than other students and commonly react by crying, withdrawal from others, and avoidance when attacked.

Craig & pepler, 1997 suggested that bulling is often tolerated and ignored in schools. Some have estimated that teachers rarely detect this problem and only intervene in 4% of all incidents. Many of the victims are called "sissies or tattle tales" by the bullies and other students, which leaves the victim vulnerable to bullies. But more important is that often teachers say the same things about the victims. The long-range effect could be a negative social effect in schools created by bullies, during their school years, and may engage in criminal and aggressive behavior after adolescence. In addition students tend to believe that bullied students are at least partly to blame for their victimization, or they may think that bulling will make victims tougher and that teasing is simply done in fun (Oliver & Hazler, 1994). Consequently, students who report such incidents believe that nothing will be done about their victimization.

Bulling prevention programs are a total school effort designed to send a message that bulling will not be accepted, or tolerated in school. There needs to be a climate of warmth and adult involvement in school sites, and educate students to recognize bulling within the school. An effective bulling prevention program requires awareness of bulling and adult involvement. This requires a commitment on the part of all adults to reduce or eliminate bulling. Effective programs have significantly reduced the occurrence of bulling and have improved school climate. Educators must act now, before more school violence and gang membership continues in the schools.

HOW SOME EXPERTS HAVE ADDRESSED THE ISSUE OF SCHOOL VIOLENCE

To answer part of this question the author has studied three professional Journals, The American Psychologist (APA Journal) and two of The Forensic Examiner journals. The first Journal quoted is, "The American Psychologist," Oct. 2001, Vol. 56 Number 10 pages 797 and 800.

Many communities have seen curriculum changes, the adoption of "safe school" policies, new weapons-reporting requirements, and increased efforts to refer problem students to mental health professionals yet adolescent deaths indicate that violent deaths are a rare event, with less than one percent of homicides and suicides among school-age children. However, as Joseph Stalin, of all people, noted in the past, "a single death is a tragedy, a million deaths is a statistic." (As quoted by Burtlett, 1990 p, 766). There now may have been enough tragedies to precipitate action. Getting accurate information about the activities of high-risk students rests heavily on establishing and maintaining a supportive school environment. Ironically, many schools appear to be taking the opposite approach. Instead of working to foster a sense of belonging, schools are implementing zero-tolerance policies that virtually guarantee an unreasoned response to any reported problem. For example, when a student is expelled or suspended for carrying aspirin (in violation of zero tolerance drug policies) that student is likely to hold the school administration in contempt. With disproportionate punishments can we really expect other students to "tell" on other students?

The following comes from two journals with the same title and they are: "The Forensic Examiner" dated May/June 1999 and May/June 2000. The May/June issue dealt with the article named, "Kids Who Kill" page 19. This article relates to the issues of "Attachment Disorders, Anti Social Personality and Violence."

Every five minutes a child is arrested for a violent crime. The average American child spends 900 hours a year in school and 1,500 hours watching TV. By the time a child leaves elementary school he or she has seen 8,000 murders and over 100,000 other acts of violence. May/June 2000. What can we expect from our youth if this is their entertainment? Since the Columbine and other school-shootings many school psychologists have been asked by administrators to conduct assessment of dangerousness on students. However, School psychologists must be careful not to make claims that they can predict behavior when assessing dangerousness the psychologist attempts to determine the potentially dangerous patterns have become firmly entrenched.

The author questions are, do the universities in the Psychology and sociology Departments have curricula addressing assessment of these kids, and are the psychologists trained or prepared to conduct such assessments? The answer is probably not. For instance, the author is the only one that taught the gang culture and school violence in Teacher Preparation. The author is concerned that too few psychologists are trained or prepared to conduct such assessments, especially for the K-6 classrooms.

The biggest problem facing our schools today is adequate funding for all programs. In the California budget for 2003 did not contain enough funding for the war on gangs and school violence. Funds are scarce to employ professionals that can help in this effort. Counselors and School Psychologists are desperately needed to combat this rising crisis. How many youngsters need to die before the schools and universities receive federal and state funding to address these important issues?

THE STUDENTS AND THE "CODE OF SILENCE" LEADING TO SCHOOL VIOLENCE

Following are what some students said about the code:

Most school shooters plan their attacks and give warning to their classmates. So why are so many kids reluctant to speak up about what they know?

"When you read about all the school shooting, the media always glorifies the killers, the people they shoot just become a bunch of statistics." Erick Wallingford a student at Santana High School as told to David Oliver Relin

"At both Columbine and Santana, it has become clear that students overheard threats and might have prevented the violence.... This reluctance may stem from a student culture that ... encourages a "code of silence." Teen People page 127

15-year-old Andy Williams had been telling friends he was thinking of "pulling a Columbine." At a local park the week before the shooting, he reportedly told a half dozen of his friends, I am going to shoot up the school on Monday." Another student later said, "How hard was anyone really trying?" If they wanted to stop it, why didn't they just talk to the principal" Teen People Page 127

Kids say that there are 3 reasons they're reluctant to speak up: 1. They don't know how to tell serious threats from jokes. 2. What adult do I go to who would deal with it properly? 3. If I tell, am I going to be branded "a rat or a narc?"

Can the code of silence be broken?

Peter Blauvelt (President of the National Alliance for safe schools. He has said (page 128) "I talk to school administrators all the time. And I tell them "you can't just expect students to come forward and speak, you have to show them you're willing to listen." If every school made it clear to students that there were a few trusted adults standing by who would keep their identities anonymous, the students would be much more willing to come forward. Students are more powerful than metal detectors in a school and if administrators were vigilant in identifying a kid that becomes enraged and also knows what to do, and know how to handle the situation.
The answer is yes!

CLOSURE

The minority communities have experienced gang violence for many years, however, little attention has been given to it by the dominant culture because it has not affected them very much except for a few "drive-bys" where some of them may have been in the wrong place at the wrong time, and also because the feelings may have been, "as long as they are killing each other, who cares."

However, school shootings has affected almost all of society and has been placed in the limelight. Why? Perhaps a few words need to be said about this phenomenon. The following Modesto Bee article can shed a light on this. The following is a paraphrase of the Modesto Bee article dated 4/15/01.

The very word "Columbine" is shorthand for a complex set of emotions ranging from anxiety to sadness to empathy. Across the nation, Columbine is cited as life's defining moment. The calamity in Littleton Colorado seems to have called young people out of themselves more than any other event that we have seen. It has taken students to a new level of awareness. They are asking, "Who am I, and what is my community like?" Students who have never had a close brush with violence may have reacted more strongly to media reports of students of similar age and background being slain at a school that reminds them of their own.

Violence has seeped into the student's daily lives and the once tranquil school has become a battle ground and now they face lock-down drills that have robbed them of what traditionally has been the carefree time of adolescence. Schools are no longer seen as guaranteed safe shelters. Seventeen year old students now see none athletes, the so-called "nerds", and some who may be called faggots in a very different light. Adolescents from all walks of life have reacted with dismay to Columbine and other shootings. Some students have said, "The school shootings have made many people aware of the reality of school violence." Yet, the violence has not ceased and leaves us to wonder, where and when will it happen again?

School and gang violence are both destructive and school administrators cannot put all their efforts on one at the expense of the other, both need to be emphasized and addressed. Society may feel that gang members and school shooters should be placed in jail, and many should be. However, there are not enough jails to incarcerate all the teen-aged gang members and school shooters at this time.

For instance, in Merced County, California Juvenile Hall, California rated its juvenile capacity as 42, in January 1998. However, the population was 48, consequently, 22 juveniles were booked then released, and 99 are still waiting to serve their sentence. This is ludicrous. Now California wants to build more jails instead of preventing youngsters from going to juvenile hall (another name for jail?) to begin with. Building more jails will be at the expense of funding for schools. It takes over $21, 000 to keep juveniles in jail and $4, 500 to keep them in school with preventative measures. Which is cheaper?

The questions remain, "How can teachers recognize a dangerous situation?" What can teachers do about it? What do they need to do in the future?" The important question here is: when will school districts cease to "lay off" the professional personnel that are desperately needed to address the school and gang violence such as school psychologists and counselors when ever a school budget is lowered?

The author's research and studies have concluded that too many people, agencies and schools are attempting to address the problem of school violence, but unfortunately they are not addressing the issues, they are simply hiding it and hope that the problem simply goes away, but it will not go away and more studies are needed and more curricula has to include the gang culture and school violence if Americans can finally address these dreadful problems in the classroom. We must not be in denial about gangs in school and school violence. However, we must be pro-active and begin to solve the problem.

Actually it is really a very simple thing to do. Therefore, the ultimate and profound suggestion to teachers is, "don't just teach subjects. Instead teach students." This means that subjects should be taught, but the student must be the primary focus and insure that all students are treated equally. If we would teach to the student's brain we could go far and remember that the brain has no color, gender, or ethnicity.

CHAPTER 6

PREVENTION OR INTERVENTION EDUCATIONAL
PROGRAMS FOR GANGS AND SCHOOL VIOLENCE

THERE IS ALWAYS HOPE

Other appropriate prevention programs are scattered in other chapters, but the following needs to be included in this chapter for clarification. This chapter begins with an article from "Urban Education" Sage Publications, 1989. The article states:

> Self proclaimed gang members differ significantly from their peers in ways that reveal their multiple marginality (Vigil, 1988). First, their socioeconomic status, determined from by parent's occupation, was lower than that of their classmates; Second they were disproportional Latino and in Los Angels Latino gang members out number the African American gang members by 3 to 1. Significantly more Latino gang members than other Latino youth spoke Spanish at home and with their best friends. In addition, gang members had less self-esteem, academic achievement, and self-confidence than their White peers. They also perceived their parents as having lower educational aspirations from them. This report explains how a majority of gang members stated that they valued education was surprising; it was surprising because many educators tend to believe that gang members are not interested in education and are dumb because they join gangs.

None of the factors mentioned here precludes the schools and teachers as the first "soldiers in the battle field" to develop alternative prevention plans because teachers get to know and understand the students and they can be the first line of defense. Consequently, the rest of the school administration and the community need to support and aid the classroom teacher. However, the teachers or other educators are seldom part of the planning, or strategy formation because law enforcement and community leaders tend to meet alone. Consequently, without input from the education community, especially the teachers, the first line of defense is left out. The K-5 teachers are involved with the wanna be gang members everyday even if they don't know they have wanna bee's in their classroom. Without the educator's input, can society really address the gang issues in the community?

GANG INTERVENTION APPROACHES; THE GOOD, THE BAD, AND THE NOT SO UGLY

1. Incarceration alone does not always work, and we can't build sufficient numbers of jails, fast enough to solve the problem. Some of the gang members also consider the prisons as PENN State University because the most powerful, knowledgeable, and experienced gang leaders are in prison, most of them for life. Consequently, if a hardcore gang member wants to learn from the best, they must go to prison, what is often considered by the gang members as, their "graduate School." The prison, or graduate school, allows gang members to learn other or better ways to commit crime or selling drugs by the "experts." This cycle continues over and over again because the parolees are paroled back to the area when they were first sent to prison. The cycle will continue until the offenders are sentenced to prison for life and then they become the "experts who will train the new comers." Consequently, are jails or prisons really the answer in the prevention of gangs and school violence? More importantly, the California taxpayers are paying for more and more prisons, or graduate schools, as they are called by gang members, and play into the gang member's game.

2. By the time the legal system actually punishes juvenile offenders, they have to long of a criminal history to turn them around. In many counties, the juvenile halls are full and there isn't enough space for many of them. They are booked into juvenile hall and promptly released. Many wait months before they are locked up and by that time many in the legal system do not know what other illegal things they have committed while waiting to do their time.

3. Most of the suppression programs, in schools, are to retaliate and the students may view this as grounds for more crime. Furthermore, those prisoners who are paroled are returned to the area they came from. Upon release their

"homies" await to take them back to the same environment that they came from.

4. Boot camps do not affect recidivism rates more favorably than other programs do for antisocial and delinquent youth.

5. Day treatment programs, with educational and rehabilitative components appear to be more effective than incarceration, but only rarely available for juvenile offenders.

6. The best time to intervene with the gang population is at school entry or in pre-school. This is when the kids can be kept form-joining gangs if students are provided an equal and unbiased education.

Realistic and Distinctive Approaches

School officials must be realistic in their approach to gangs and decide whether to concentrate their efforts on preventing or reducing gang related activities. The term prevention implies that methods can be employed to remove evidence of gangs and negative gang activities at school. Reduction implies that methods can be employed to lessen the effect of negative gang activities. The suggested prevention strategies in the following discussions also have relevance as reduction strategies.

Administrators who deny the presence of gangs limit their options to confront gangs realistically and effectively. In studying Detroit gangs, Taylor (1988) recognized that school administrators were victims of the "ostrich syndrome" when they became defensive and ignored critical problems at their schools. Lal (1991) also found that in denying negative situations (such as gang activity and school violence) school officials exacerbated the problem. Reluctance by officials to address the gang issue on campus is primarily due to a lack of knowledge about gangs, or leads to stereotypes of the youth. Once school officials acquire the knowledge and transcend the denial stage by adopting a realistic perspective, they can initiate, maintain, and evaluate solution strategies. Following is a suggestion by Lal:

Administrators who are most successful in their efforts to confront negative gang activities are those who develop a site-specific approach to the problem. In doing so, a distinctive leadership style emerges that permits officials to possess a certain mentality (attitude) about gangs. Similar to the gang mentality of most gang members, which in essence holds that nothing is more important than the gang, and members are willing to do whatever the gang demands, so too must school officials adopt a "positive school mentality." Administrators must believe that nothing is more important than providing a safe school environment for students and staff members, and be willing to do whatever is necessary to prevent, or reduce the negative effects of gang activity on campus. However, unlike the gangs, this mentality must not diminish the value of the individual student as a human being. "You accept the person. You do not accept the disruptive behavior" (Lal et al., 1993, p.44).

Taking a distinctive approach encourages the development of an organizational framework for the school's gang prevention program. There are various ways to organize site-specific solution strategies, and school officials must decide what is most beneficial for their school sites. Regardless of the organizational design, constant revisions of strategies will be necessary. They should be adaptable because of the vacillating behavioral patterns of gangs. The following sections discuss three categories of solution strategies: operational strategies, alternative behavior strategies, and engagement strategies. (Alternatively, for a comprehensive narrative of organizing solutions based on two categories, primary and secondary strategies, Lal et al., 1993, pp. 44-53.)

Operational Strategies

Operational strategies direct the operation or processes of the program. Initially, the principal sets the tone for change and employs key personnel to assist with operational or organizational tasks. Later this core group (including the principal) may be expanded to a team that will assume responsibility for all program elements. Development of this process will depend on the individual situations at each school. The following operational strategies have conventional applications for a variety of campus circumstances. The following ideas are suggested for implementation in school districts and at school sites where gang and school violence may erupt at any time, in fact they should be implemented to prevent negative behaviors at a school.

1. Create a positive environment by developing a school philosophy about gangs.
2. Assemble a support team and delineate tasks. Establish a communications network
3. Analyze the school and community environments.
4. Formulate realistic goals and objectives.
5. Enact school policy related to gang activity. The focus must be "prevention" rather than punishment.
6. Maintain school security for students and staff.
7. Coordinate the development of all solution strategies.
8. Provide for continuous evaluation and modification.

Creating a positive environment is no simple task. As the school leader, the principal is ultimately accountable for the entire educational process and the cultural climate of the school. Bringing about change, while cultivating the commitment of school personnel, students, and parents, will require dedication and skill. This process will not occur overnight and is not a single effort. Just as the gangs proceed through an evolutionary process, schools in transition must also experience evolutionary development.

School officials attempting to create a positive school climate must possess certain characteristics and engage in specific behaviors and activities, just as gang members do. Administrators must be unfailing in their convictions (but flexible), practice the dynamic and enthusiastic behaviors of a positive leadership style, and be actively involved in all aspects of the program (Lal, et al., 1993)

One of the first activities for the administrator is establishing the school's "gang" philosophy. Gangs have an unwritten philosophy (gang code) that all members comprehend and adhere to (i.e., nothing is more important than the gang). Similarly, the school's gang philosophy or code should be understood by all, aligned with the school's overall philosophy, publicized, and guide all elements of the program. Lal et al. (1993) offered the following example:

The school campus should be a neutral and safe place. The only gang allowed on site is the (name of school) gang. All students belong to our gang. It is the family. Negative and disruptive gang behaviors will not be tolerated on this campus. Members will not be ostracized simply because they are members, but will be treated equally and fairly. If members engage in unacceptable behavior, they will be subject to disciplinary action.

Assembling a support team requires knowledge about the faculty and skill in assigning tasks. It is critical that staff not be coerced into performing certain tasks simply because of a job description. Often the person best suited for a specific task, such as gathering information about the gangs on campus, is a person with ties to the community rather than the administrator in charge of discipline. Because selection of team members is highly related to program tasks, membership recruitment criteria should include levels of expertise (all members will eventually obtain an adequate knowledge base of the gangs), willingness and readiness to complete assigned tasks, and interpersonal relationship skills.

Students are often overlooked as resources; administrators would be wise to investigate the possibility of including students (gang and non-gang members) on the team. The following is a suggested pairing of team members to various tasks.

1. The principal (or team coordinator) should adhere or develop inventories, available resources and facility operations, reviews policy, schedules, and assignments, and establishes program parameters.

2. The administrator in charge of discipline (or designee): reviews school discipline records of suspected gang members, documents the number and types of gangs and their activities, checks for patterns that offer clues to gang activity.

3. The appearance of gangs in the school sites should trigger a comprehension of the underlying intentions of gang activity and will assist school personnel in developing specific strategies and enacting policy to counteract their occurrences.

THE FOLLOWING LIST OF ACTIVITIES WERE FORMED BY OTHER AGENCIES, BUT ARE VALUABLE AND ARE LISTED BELOW

Gang Activity	Intention of action
Graffiti	Communicating, warning, and marking Turf
Flashing/Slanging Hanging out	Claiming affiliation, identifying, threats
Relaxing	Marking turf and show of force, protection for members,
Intimidation	Gaining control, gaining respect, instilling fear
Recruitment	Building a power base, establishing loyalties, and sustaining membership
Extortion	Instilling fear, gaining respect, and getting easy money
Assaults/Fights	Courting-in/out, retaliation, gaining respect, by show of force
Drug use/dealing	Acquiring money, getting high, partying
Use/Sale of weapons	protecting self, members, turf, drug traffic, acquiring money

SUMMARY OF OTHER CHAPTERS, INDICATORS OF POSSIBLE GANG INVOLVEMENT, IDEAS FOR PREVENTION, OR WHEN TO TAKE ACTION: INFORMATION FOR PARENTS AND SCHOOL PERSONAL

1. Changes in the child's behavior.
2. Not associating with long-time friends and being secretive about new friends and activities.
3. Changes in hair or dress style and/or having a group of friends with the same hair or dress style.
4. Changes in normal routines with new friends, such as not coming home after school or staying out late without giving explanation.
5. Suspected drug use.
6. Unexplained material possessions, such as expensive clothing or jewelry.
7. Presence of firearms, ammunition, or other deadly weapons.
8. Change in attitude about school, church, or other normal activities.
9. Discipline problems at school, church, or other attended activities.
10. Lower grades in school or skipping school.
11. Increase in confrontational behavior, such as talking back, verbal abuse, name calling, and disrespect for parental authority.
12. A new fear of police.
13. Phone threats to the family by other rival gangs, or unknown callers directed at person involved in gangs.
14. Graffiti on or around your residence-in your kid's room, on note books, furniture, clothing, etc.
15. Physical signs of having been in a fight-bruises, cuts, etc.
16. A new found sense of bravery- he or she may brag that they are too tough to be "messed with."
17. Use of a new nickname.
18. Tattoos or "branding" with gang-related symbols.

Note: Items 1-18 were taken from: "A community Response to Street Gangs," prepared by the Kansas City, Missouri Police Department and Gang Squad

IDENTIFYING AND DOCUMENTING GANG MEMBERS

Cooperation between the school and law enforcement personnel ensures the effectiveness of identification strategies. Identifying and documenting the gang population in school and in the community are continuous and evolving processes, because gang membership is transitory. The following basic steps of identification strategies require intelligence gathering type tactics such as:

surveillance, investigation, and documentation. Surveillance tactics involve the observation of:

(a) Locations where groups of students congregate, mill, hang out, or get high.

(b) Signs of graffiti at these locations, an indication that the group is claiming or has claimed that territory;

(c) Patterns of movement, as the group move or roam from place to place,

(d) Peculiar behaviors of individual group members, such as their stance, walk, speech, and actions like flashing gang signs and yelling out gang slogans;

(e) Evidence of gang paraphernalia, such as caps with team insignia, rags hanging out of pockets, graffiti on personal belongings; See chapter on team hats, and

(f) Physical appearance, such as scars, tattoos, hairstyles, and pierced body parts.

In the initial investigation stages it may not be clear who the gang members are, so it would be prudent to identify any groups and group members who gather together. This process allows school administrators (and those who assist with the investigation) opportunities to become familiar with members of the gangs as well as other students. Investigation techniques also facilitate the discovery of associations between gangs, their members, and their activities.

Investigation tactics for group identification entail:

(a) Ascertaining names of gangs by speaking with law enforcement personnel, community members, ex-gang members, and other students. However, confidentiality is paramount so as not to place a student in any danger,

(b) Determining type of gang (newly formed, delinquent, or violent) by observing and making inquires about their activities;

(c) Making connections between the gangs and their claimed territories by noticing if members occupy the same location daily; and

(d) Noticing possible gang paraphernalia, such as certain colors, style of dress, and graffiti.

(e) Identifying members by their given name and their gang nickname-moniker or placa, the placa usually appears in graffiti,

(f) Classifying members as either wanna bee (those who are hanging around and romancing the gang), peripheral, affiliate, or hard-core informants may not be reliable). Law enforcement and community agencies that encounter gangs on a daily basis are the most reliable verification sources and can supply additional information to a database. Available resources and personnel expertise will determine methods of data storage. Effective methods have key descriptors (coded), cross-referencing, built-in updating features, and protected access as essential components. Never ID informants without using the code usage.

Whether the data is stored in computer files or handwritten logs, certain information is critical (but all of it is not necessary to initiate the record; information can be added at any time). For example, in making gang associations, list the name of the gang, its known members and those who hang around it; classify the gang (i.e., delinquent) and members (i.e., affiliate); provide samples of paraphernalia and graffiti (placas); identify their claimed territory; and list activities the gang has engaged in at school and in the community. Records of individual members include vital statistics such as the student's name, address, phone number, name of parent or guardian, class schedule, gang affiliation, and moniker. Photographs of members and graffiti on buildings, walls, desks, books, etc., provide an additional sources of identification.

Another documentation tool is the student profile, as an assimilation profile. School personnel update and evaluate student progress in the profile at regularly scheduled intervals. These profiles should be discussed with the students because the files are a "permanent file that could follow the student's" for the rest of their lives and this could lead them to a life of crime, or death. Profiles have the same key elements, and contain all of the data noted in the identification file, plus this additional information:

1. Academic progress, attendance patterns, and disciplinary matters

2. Recruitment to and/or involvement in school clubs or activities.

3. Record of all conferences (note significant results).

4. Notations of class schedule changes and reasons for the change.

As part of the documentation process, inform members that they are being investigated, that a file on them is being maintained, and that they and their activities are being monitored. Above all, notify the students that if these files contain an overabundance of negative behavior they will be compounded if they are incorporated with a criminal record and school files can become very important when an individual goes to court on felony or criminal charges.

Building Interpersonal Relationships With Gang Members

Building rapport with students is an arduous process, and requires special skills usually linked to the leadership or operational style of the adult. Cultivating the necessary skills to interact with gang members may be difficult, but not impossible. Revisiting the reasons for gang membership will facilitate this task. Members are attracted to a gang because it satisfies certain social and emotional needs not found in the family, society at large, or in the school environment. A review of school records and discussions with teachers, family members, and significant others provide clues for approaching and interacting with individual members.

Learning the names of members is necessary before any attempts at building rapport can begin. Most students, gang and non-gang affiliated, feel a sense of importance when adults at school call them by name. Maintaining the distinction of the adult position and demanding respect at all times while interacting with the members is essential. Members do not need another buddy; they already have each other. However, they do need a person who can assist in their transformation from a gang member who engages in unacceptable and antisocial behavior to a person who is accepted by the society at large.

It has been found that regular contact and communication with gang members are most successful in informal settings, for instance, when hanging out in their claimed territory, but keep it in mind that you are not one of them. Dialogues with members at regular intervals and in various situations also support a wide range of relationships between members and school personnel, just as interaction among members during milling periods promotes camaraderie.

Usually most schools have an abundance of human resources. The principal and/or other administrators need to find and include the most appropriate people for special projects to address the gang problem. Those staff members who reside within the school neighborhood and are familiar with gangs are valuable and should be encouraged to assist with project elements. Interpersonal relationship with Parents and Other Family Members is vital, especially parents and family members who have gang involved youngsters and who have varying attitudes about gangs. It is up to educators to educate themselves about their children if they are gang affiliated and give parents the information needed to reduce or stop the child from becoming a hard-core gang member. It is, however, the school's responsibility to supply parents with Information that will help them help their child. Parents should be told that their child is gang-affiliated and explain consequences for gang involvement.

Community Members

Community resources in gang-infested neighborhoods may be sparse because they tend to live in a depressed socio-economically area. However, there may be federal money available to overcome this defect and encourage community members to participate at no cost to them. Community membership in prevention programs is crucial and all efforts need to be planned to include them.

Many programs whose purpose is to prevent violence, or inappropriate behavior are also programs that might prevent disaffection, dropping out of school, drug and alcohol abuse, and poor academic performance. In other words, many prevention-oriented interventions are interventions that are not specific to violence or behavior and address universals that affect a variety of possible negative outcomes related to schooling.

School climate might be defined as the feelings that students and staff have about the school environment over a period of time. These feelings may have to do with how comfortable each individual feels in the environment and whether the individual feels that it is supportive of learning, or teaching is appropriately organized and is safe. Climate may also address other positive or negative feelings regarding the school environment.

Therefore, the school climate is a reflection of the positive, or negative feelings regarding the school environment and it may directly or indirectly affect a variety of learning outcomes. The author's summary is that all of these surveys can be found out by conducting on-going surveys of staff, teachers and students. Many surveys have identified three components to a comprehensive approach to violence prevention in schools. These include:

a) Prevention,
b) Identification and intervention for students at risk or having difficulty,
c) Effective responses once inappropriate behavior has occurred.

Although all three components must be implemented simultaneously and effectively in a truly comprehensive approach, the focus here is on the first of these components, basic prevention. All programs that focus on basic prevention of violence, drug abuse, dropping out, or whatever, also focus on creating a positive school climate. Effective intervention requires a wide spectrum of options that move significantly beyond a narrow focus on punishment and exclusion, which themselves can contribute to a negative school climate. Security measures intended to reduce school crime may be positive to some, but negative for others

Mentoring programs, peer-and cross-age tutoring programs, school-within-a-school programs, cooperative learning, home base/homeroom programs, looping in which teachers advance grade levels each year to remain with students, programs emphasizing welcoming and belonging in schools. All probably have a role in violence prevention as a result they have not been viewed as violence-prevention programs. Perhaps they should be viewed that way.

Traditionally, parents in involvement roles have been limited to activities such as parent-teacher organizational meetings and parent teacher conferences. However, parents should be involved in other activities such as, providing opportunities for volunteering to increase parental involvement so that parents may develop a degree of "ownership" that could include decision-making in planning the academic curriculum. Parents could also collaborate-with-community components and use community resources to strengthen school programs. Studies have shown that parent involvement is positively associated with student success, higher attendance rates, and lower suspension rates.

Increased parent involvement has shown that it leads to greater teacher satisfaction, improved parent understanding and parent-child communication, and more successful and effective school programs. Schools can encourage parent involvement in a number of ways including parenting, learning at home, two way communications, volunteerism, and decision-making. Specifics for most programs may vary. However, parent-school collaboration will promote healthy-child/student development and a safe school environment.

All of these ideas can only be effective if teachers, administrators, school boards, parents and the teacher's union are working together, and that they are on the same task if school violence is to be prevented. Many scholars suggest various ways to prevent school violence. However, if the school board is not supportive, and the site administrators are not supportive, nothing will happen. If the teacher's unions are left out of the picture, no ideas, no matter how well planned, will not be implemented if the teachers and their union will only see prevention as just another task leveled at the overworked teacher.

PREVENTION MEASURES FOR SCHOOL VIOLENCE

The following information comes from CPA Briefings, December 2001; the first briefing is by California Attorney General, Bill Lockyer and the second by Dr. Dunbar.

As the reader will learn, from these articles, about school violence in schools, prevention is much more difficult than it is for gangs. However, the following information will present some ideas that may lead toward prevention of school violence, but the information needs to be read and studied very carefully before plans for prevention are formulated. It is clear to see, by reading these "briefs" that the selection of professional people and agencies, involved in any prevention plan must be carefully selected, or we risk not addressing the issue of school violence, or more importantly, we may do all the wrong things. This would cause much work, false hope, and in the end nothing will be accomplished, except for developing many unhappy people.

Effective crime prevention strategies must start with children who are exposed to violence. We know unless we intervene, children exposed to violence in their own families and neighborhoods will suffer devastating consequences. One in every four California children is directly exposed to violence as a victim, or witness. The National Institute of Justice reports that, on average, abused and neglected children begin committing crimes at younger ages and commit nearly twice as many offences as non-abused children. Fortunately, combing new science pertaining to mental health and brain development with traditional law enforcement and social services is helping us lead the way to a brighter future. (Atty. General Lockyer quotes, Dr. Bruce Perry, Chief of Psychiatry at Texas Children's Hospital.)

In the same conference, Dr. Perry suggests that children with effective resolution of violence requires early intervention that respects the integrity and dignity of all concerned. In order to establish safe schools, school personnel need to be increasingly aware of the nature and implications of violence upon schools and should be trained in ways to deal effectively with that violence. In the same "briefings" Dr. Dunbar, a clinical psychology professor at UCLA in an article at briefings, "youth violence": an evolving Area for Psychological Intervention can offer a more balanced and realistic approach to what can be done to help at-risk students, he also States that, In an age in which many parents turn to media-appointed experts such as James Dobson and Laura Schlessinger, psychologists can offer a more balanced and realistic approach to what can be done to help at-risk kids. For too long the field of applied psychology has been divided on the issue of prediction of future violence in general and by young men in particularly, the usual suspects, literally and figuratively, in most crime in America. Effective evaluation of violence in children and adolescents is a critical issue in keeping our schools and communities safe. The predictable response of many academic psychologists is that clinicians are apt to produce numerous "false positives" in identifying risk for violence in conduct-disordered youth. Yet, forensic psychologists know that there has been significant improvement in how risk (verses prediction) of future violence is now understood. The assessment of psychopaths, and actuarial-based risk assessment can aid clinicians evaluating potentially violent youth. In spite of a growing body of literature that suggests psychopathic offenders can be identified during adolescence, we don't have a systematic protocol for this special class of offender. It is suggested that we are still probably a few (or more) years away from a truly valid measure of psychopaths that can begin to compare to the assessment approach of the Hare adult scales.

Dr. Dunbar also stated:

I have personally seen cases where school administrators have seriously underestimated risk. By using these empirically derived tools, advocating for appropriate services for highly at-risk students to no psychologists. At the same time, practitioners concerned with youth violence may be called upon to help school personnel think more clearly about what does and does not constitute risk for violence in their student body. Dr. Dunbar quotes Randy Borum, a forensic researchers, by saying, (Borum) has noted the problem encountered by criminologists and policy makers in trying to produce a composite of school shooters. Borum has noted that the demographic and behavioral profiles proposed by the FBI do not accurately describe the shooters. Psychologists need to stress how little is known about young men who are likely to engage in acts of mass violence. It falls upon psychologists to provide a more complex understanding of violence risk than the trench coat mafia stereotype of the Columbine perpetrators.

Too frequently school administrators, law enforcement, and directors of public agencies see all mental health treatment-and all mental health providers-as interchangeable. Some of these folks are open to understanding the importance of differences in our interventions, whereas some are frankly disinterested. Likewise, I have seen how managed care services deal with highly at-risk youth via provision of minimal services. It is important to make clear to parents and other stakeholders what does and does not constitute effective treatment for potentially violent adolescents.

Promising Therapeutic Interventions

A very convincing model of comprehensive treatment of at-risk youth is found in Multisystemic Therapy (MST). MST is an intensive family and community based treatment that addresses the multiple determinants of serious antisocial and violent behaviors of highly at-risk youth in a number of federally supported studies.

Our communities need to hear from psychological practitioners who are informed about current research and treatment findings concerning prevention of youth violence, and its assessment and treatment. Our input can help educators design and evaluate interventions in schools and communities. It falls on us to advocate against the minimal aka useless-psychotherapy offerings that managed care firms try to foist on distressed families.

In closing this chapter the author has addressed the issue of "prevention" for gangs, and school violence and other youngsters who are involved in deviant behavior. The author certainly hopes that his suggestions and ideas will be considered, and becomes part of the schools policies and that the information becomes collaboration with other affected agencies. If America does not act now in the prevention of gang and school violence, they will escalate and the youngsters will be the losers, if not dead!

CHAPTER 7

PEDAGOGY TO DETER SCHOOL AND GANG VIOLENCE: AN ACADEMIC PREVENTION PROGRAM

This chapter presents one suggestion of an academic program that can be implemented in the classroom. However, there are many others that can be implemented. Which ever program is used it must be one that focuses on the learner and not on the academic/core programs. Moreover, the author strongly suggests that all academic, or core subjects be interrelated and not taught in isolation from each other. This means that if the subject of the hour is math then math ought to include reading, science. Social studies, and PE. For example reading can be reading of math books related to ethnic minorities, which includes social studies; then science is included by an explanation of how science makes sense of math, and measuring the speed and distance from the classroom to the rear fence of the schoolyard can include PE. All of these suggestions are listed toward the end of this chapter. However, teachers ought to remember that the learners are the focus and not the subject called "reading." as can be seen, this pedagogy program is effective for all students, but it is most effective to prevent violence in the schools.

The state of the art for teaching children in California, as well as other states is that education is under mandates for school reform and accountability that can only be demonstrated by testing children. In California the race for school improvement and the threat of the State taking over low performance schools, after a period of time, to improve them, has led the school districts to prepare the students for the state "test." This means the teachers may have to "teach the test" and very little time is left to "teach children." This is a tragedy for the teachers and the students because schools end up producing children that are well prepared to pass a test, but who have learned very little and not prepared for "real life." The author hopes that the federal and state governments stay out of the education business and let the professional teachers do what they do best---Teach. California is even worse off because there is an elected "Secretary of Education" and the governor has his own appointed Secretary of Education. Why? California is still at the bottom of the educational ladder, so why does it have two secretaries while the state is financially BROKE.

The author attends many conferences where he presents math and science teaching strategies. During a math presentation at a conference, the author was told, "what you are presenting is fantastic, but you don't understand that the kids still have to pass a test so we don't have time to teach what you are presenting." My response was, "if the kids learn and understand math, they will be empowered to pass any math test."

Unfortunately, schools are creating students that don't understand math, or for that matter most other subjects. On the other hand teachers who teach, normally teach subject matter instead of teaching children. This means that the content is emphasized instead of emphasizing the student's learning styles. Moreover, teachers should teach subjects so that students learn math, science and other subjects that relate to real life situations rather than teach them theories in isolation from real life.

As has been stated in the other chapters, gang members are not dumb and they do appreciate an education, but they do not agree on how education is delivered in the classrooms to them. In this chapter the author is attempting to provide ideas on how education can be delivered to prevent gang membership and school violence. It is his premise that if the ideas presented here are implemented then gangs and school violence can be significantly reduced and hopefully some day these negative factors can become insignificant. If we do not change the way students are taught we will continue the path of denial.

Consequently, in this chapter the author provides ideas and methods that will place the focus on the students and not the subject matter. He will also attempt to show how all subjects are interrelated and that subjects taught should include all other subjects instead of subjects taught in isolation. For more than a century educators we have been concerned with SURFACE KNOWLEDGE instead of teaching MEANINGFUL KNOWLEDGE. We may not have considered the difference, but without thinking we have been involved in teaching surface knowledge. What is meant by this? The overwhelming need of learners is learning for knowledge and there are two basis of knowledge. One is called Surface Knowledge and it involves memorization of facts and procedures. Yes some memorization is important. But surface knowledge is anything a robot can do. It refers to programming and to memorization of the "mechanics" of any subject. Tragically, surface knowledge isn't even taught today because the teachers are forced to "teach to the test" that all students are required to pass in the name of "accountability."

The other method is called Meaningful Knowledge and is critical for success in the 21st. century. This knowledge is anything that makes sense to the learner. Understanding a subject results from perceiving relationships and the function of educators is to provide our students with the experiences that enable them to perceive the patterns that connect. However, most testing is geared toward recognizing surface knowledge. Teachers must remember that gang members use both surface and meaningful knowledge when they teach other gang members the math they need to sell drugs and the street language needed to succeed as gang members. On the other hand teachers usually teach only surface knowledge. Hence, gang members are ahead of the general public and teachers because the gang leadership teaches what a member needs to sell drugs. Unfortunately, the theories learned in university methods classes lead teachers to the following assumptions.

ADDRESSING SOME ASSUMPTIONS IN EDUCATION

ASSUMPTION ONE: "THE FACTORY MODEL" 64

In traditional factories, products are manufactured on an assembly line, and the final product is the combination of readily identifiable parts that are made using precisely measurable materials. Work is done according to specific schedules, with precise times for beginning, taking breaks, and ending (when the bell rings). Speed, accuracy, and the amount of output are rewarded. Similarly, in most schools, we still find that subjects are taught separately. The students then move through subjects in an assembly-line routine. Times and places for learning and recess are specifically allocated according to the need to cover subject matter-instead of teaching according to a student's needs and thirst for knowledge. And just as content is predetermined, so are outcomes specified in terms of general standards, skills, and facts, which make it relatively easy to test for success

ASSUMPTION 2 "BEHAVIORISM" 65

The factory model provides fertile ground for the "behavioral" approach to learning, which has dominated educational practices for over 50 years. It is an approach predicated on the beliefs that what we learn can be reduced to specific, readily identifiable parts and that equally identifiable rewards and punishments can be used to "produce" the desired learning. According to some scholars Skinner was wrong.

When others control rewards and punishments, for students, most children will look to others for direction and answers. Therefore, their innate search for meaning is short-circuited. Another consequence is that they are actually deprived of major rewards such as the joy and excitement that are the consequences of real learning. When all options are determined in advance, students are actually deprived of the opportunity to do some of the innovative and creative things that are essential for adequate learning. That forces them back into memorization of tests.

ASSUMPTION 3: "THE NEEDS OF THIS MODERN GENERATION"

"Many things have happened in this century, and most of them plug into walls." One function of school is to prepare students for the real world. The assumption is that the schools do meet this goal. The reality is that it does not. In fact it fosters illusions and obscures the real challenges. In particular, it fails to deal with the impact of electronic media. Children growing up with "electronic miracles" are different and teachers need new patterns of defense, perception, understanding, and evaluation. Teachers need a new kind of education! Yet many schools are not preparing the students to cope with and take charge of the influences of technology and the media and they should be.

What price does society pay for adhering to these assumptions? The students are more than machines. The question of capacity looks very different if teachers consider it from the perspective of biology rather than of engineering. If teachers regard the mind as something living and growing rather than a machine our teaching methods would change. The problem is that the assumptions discussed here conspire to have learners treated as machines and to severely inhibit effective education and the functioning of the students' brains.

Educators cannot afford to stay in the memorization business. They must redefine their role and become generators of meaningful, connecting, and linking knowledge, that can not only use the computer "SOFTWARE," but that they can surpass its performance. If educators don't the future looks bleak. Society must believe in the power of teachers, and also believe that they can empower students. BRAIN based learning focuses heavily on the teacher as the major facilitator of learning. But real facilitating, which engages more abilities and capacities of the human brain, will require much more than the level of teaching that has become the standard in most of the schools.

Society and educators must address the above issues with all their vigor, or risk presiding over the total collapse of public education in America. We must remember that we can not expect students to learn science by reading textbooks and memorizing definitions and formulas, no more than we can expect them to learn to play the piano by having them memorize music notes.

INTRODUCTION TO SOME BRAIN THEORIES AS RELATED TO LEARNING AND TEACHING

If teachers teach to the children's brain then they don't have to concern themselves with ethnicity, student's color, or gender. The brain can be programmed to accomplish many things and teachers can program the brain to accomplish positive outcomes. Teachers can teach to the brain if they consider the following information and implement it in their classrooms. But first the teachers need to understand the historical development of the brain and how the student's learning style determines how they learn and this should guide the teacher's teaching style to teach students. Usually teachers teach using one teaching style, or the way they were taught in college and this means that some of the students can't learn as efficiently as the one's who's style is used to learn.

THE THREE BRAINS AND THEIR FUNCTIONS

The Hindbrain is at least 200 million years old. The author realizes that some Christian religions may not adhere to these dates and we remind them that, "for God one day is like a thousand years, and a thousand years are like one day." In other words we may believe that God does operate on our earthly time. However, God operates in a different time line that is not related to the human's earthly timeline!"
(2 Peter chapter 3: verses 8-15)

This is the oldest and most primitive part of the brain. It causes us to be alert which requires the use of the five senses, Look, smell, hear, sound, taste, and feeling. It cannot deal with words, but it takes account of intimidating stares, vocal inflections, and all types of body language. It is the gatekeeper of information and no matter how brilliant our ideas or how eloquent our words, they do not stand a chance if we do not consider this part of the brain because it selects the information to be absorbed. It is also responsible for deep behavioral characteristics shared by all students. It is beneath conscious communication and causes primitive urges that teachers must address. Educators used to think that, "what we said was more important than how we said it" was before we learned how the brain functions. For children to learn: This part of the brain must be attended to so that the hindbrain allows information to be processed in the total brain.

Consequently, teachers need to make their presentations INTERESTING. But the word "interesting" does not stand-alone; it has to be interesting to the students and not just to the teacher. To teach effectively they must connect with this hindbrain and insure the students that they are trust worthy, likable and warm. If they don't reach the students emotionally, they will tune teachers out, no matter how good their facts are. If teachers think of teaching as a logical, and analytical they will lose many of the students that don't learn in this method and they must feel that the teachers can be trusted. Therefore, it is not what teachers say, but how they say it.

II THE MIDDLE BRAIN:

The middle brain develops, around the information that is monitored by the hindbrain. This part of the brain monitors emotions, such as, likes, dislikes, love, and hate. Consequently, it is the source of emotional behavior and it is the source of love and passion, but it is not controlled, nor affected by logic.

III THE FORE BRAIN

The fore brain is called the new brain because it is only a few million years old. This is the newest of the human's evolving brain. It surrounds the two earlier brains. The Fore Brain performs the highest functions of abstract thought and language. It takes in information, interprets, and analyses the information, associates this information with other information, and prepares all this for some type of outcome. It is the part of the brain that teachers should be concerned with so that they can get students to learn, think, solve problems, and to create. This part of the brain is wonderful, but it does not possess infinite knowledge because it needs to be programmed (like a computer) in order to operate efficiently. The fore brain is composed of the right and left hemispheres, in this book they will be interchanged with right and left-brains.

The brain is the processor and our senses are the inputs to our brain. The nervous system and the brain act as a unit because it involves memory and is affected by emotional and cultural factors. Children's senses, like their brains are limited. In other words the teachers model of the world is not the same as the model of the world, shared by the students, because each student has a brain filled with different information and procedures. The human sensors differ in sensitivity to given situations, or each of us programs our computer differently. Teachers and school administrators ought to be cognizant of the brain function because this may be one reason why kids join gangs-they are frustrated with the class information that is presented in a way that they can't, or won't process in their brains.

Let us remember that the human brain is responsible for Beethoven's 9th Symphony, computers, W. W. II and Hitler, Hamlet, crime, gangs, and school violence. People's brain has always defined the educational profession, yet educators have not really understood it or paid much attention to it. Understanding the brain mechanisms and processes adds an exciting dimension to people's thoughts about the teaching profession.

Let us also keep in mind that knowing 'why,' generally leads to knowing' how to. The teaching profession orientation has long been in the social and behavioral science, and few teachers understood biology, chemistry, and cognitive psychology, subjects needed to study the brain. Consequently, we have become a profession of BEHAVIORISTS, whether we liked it or not. We learned how to manipulate the student's environment to achieve the desired outcome.

However, the practical base of the teaching profession was probably closer to folklore knowledge than scientific knowledge. Teachers could predict what would probably occur in the classroom, but they generally didn't know why it occurred. They also did not understand the underlying mechanisms that govern other significant teaching and learning concerns, such as emotion, interest, attention, thinking, memory, and skill development- although teachers did learn how to address the outward behavior. Thus, studying student behavior was professionally useful, but we knew intuitively that behavior was only part of a much larger picture. Deep down, teachers could never be sure if students learned because of their efforts, or in spite of them. Teachers accepted this blind spot as a limitation of their profession.

The education profession is now at a crossroads. Educators can continue to focus their energies on the careful observation of external behavior-a course that may be adequate for managing relatively mild learning disorders-or they can join the search for a scientific understanding of the brain mechanisms, processes, and malfunctions that effect the successful completion of complex learning tasks. In this chapter the author may not provide a complete scientific understanding of the brain's mechanisms, processes, and malfunctions, however, he can use some limited knowledge as a vehicle to begin rethinking on how teachers can teach the students in the future.

The humans brain functions because both sides work complementary and simultaneously and each side collaborates with the other side and shares information of what the hemispheres perceive with each other. However, as humans will we tend to prefer one hemisphere over the other. The left side of the brain is known as the VERBAL side (abstract), and the right side is known as the PICTURING (concrete) side. Teachers should always ask themselves do students learn better with words or with pictures and hands on methods?

Those students who are at home in the "world of words", those are the ones who prefer the left-brained mode of perception, verbal, logical, and analytical, find the educational system relatively easy. Those student's who favor the right-brain mode of perception, pictures, music, and spatial design, often find the educational system quite difficult for them to succeed. To compound the FELONY the verbal "survivors" put a label on the non-survivors instead of upon the educational methodology where the real problem lies! Let us now look at KNOWLEDGE to get a better grasp of the brain.

The brain has always been a mystery to common people, but there is much that can be learned about it. Perhaps the best way of beginning this section is by describing dichotic pairs of words that have been attributed to the hemispheres to denote their separate functions. We begin by comparing a few descriptors that several researchers have discussed. Before proceeding with the specialized research used to substantiate hemispheric function, some terms need to be defined because they are used throughout the chapter. Other authors have arranged and the author has rearranged the following lists so that the dichotic pairs can project comparisons and opposites. SOME BRAIN CHARACTERISTICS

Left Hemisphere	Right Hemisphere
1. Ego	1. Super ego, Id
2. order	2. image
3. logic	3. relational
4. time & history	4. space, eternity,
5. write	5. draw
6. verbal	6. visual, non-verbal
7. analytic	7. analogic, gestalt, aesthetic
8. reason	8. fantasy, emotional
9. read/speak	9. sing
10. plan	10. dream
11. symbolic	11. visual-spatial
12. day	12. night
13. intellectual	13. sensuous, intuitive,
14. right (side of body)	14. left (side of body)
15. sequential	15. simultaneous
16. cognitive	16. affective, cooperative
17. scientific	17. humanistic
18. abstract	18. concrete
19. inductive	19. deductive

After looking at these lists of characteristics of right and left hemispheric functions, one can begin to see some general specializations.

1. The left hemisphere is seen as the side of the brain concerned with facts and figures while the right side of the brain is concerned with the meaning and spatial configuration. Although each hemisphere shares the potential for many functions and both sides collaborate in most activities; in the normal person, the two hemispheres tend to specialize. The left hemisphere is predominantly involved in analytic, logical thinking, especially in verbal, and mathematical functions for which words are an excellent tool. Its primary mode of operation is linear and it processes information sequentially. This operation, by necessity, must underlie logical thought, because logic depends on sequence and order. Language and math, both left side activities also depend on linear time. It sequentially analyzes sensory in puts, it abstracts out the relevant details, and attaches verbal labels. It looks at parts themselves; therefore, it is proficient in examining details and the relationships between them. It contains the necessary capacity for skills involved

in reading, writing, speaking, spelling, science and mathematical calculation and it has large learning capacity and memory capacities.

2. In describing the <u>right hemisphere</u> functions, one can say that it operates in a holistic or gestalt mode, and controls our orientation in space, artistic endeavors of all kinds, body image, and the ability to recognize faces and interpret facial expressions. It processes information more diffusely than the left hemisphere. It can integrate many inputs at once and is, therefore, simultaneous in its mode of operation. It is relational and has limited ability to deal with language. The right hemisphere controls visual-spatial tasks and it attends to the overall configuration of the stimulus situation. The right hemisphere is viewed as giving spatial context to the detailed analysis carried out by the left-brain. It is capable of understanding complex definitions, and is excellent in sorting out and categorizing shapes, sizes, and textures. It sees parts as having meaning only within a context. It has a limited capacity for visual word recognition and can perform only the simplest rote calculations, but can perform tasks involving spatial relations and musical patterns. The right hemisphere emphasizes integration and non-verbal awareness, is sensitive to form, both in the field of space and in the world of sound. It shows foresight, organization, and is the intuitive and mystical side, specializing in hunches. It has learning and memory capabilities; it senses, perceives, and conceptualizes. Emotions are initiated in the right hemisphere.

Perhaps two examples can clarify the two hemispheres. One, It is often said that some people see the forest and not the trees and other people see the tree (parts of the tree) and not the forest. Two, Mel Tillis used to stutter when talking (left hemisphere), but when he sang he did not stutter (right hemisphere).

As can be seen, each, "hemisphere" specializes in many functions. Although the right and left hemispheres share some part in most activities, one or the other hemisphere is the "dominant" one for any given task. Consequently, the author says that teachers should relate to teaching to the brain because the brain isn't related to ethnicity, color of skin, gang membership, or gender. The brain has none of these factors. However, this also means that standardized tests are for left brained thinkers and the other students do poorly on these tests. How does all this relate to students learning and accountability that many politicians are stressing?

Because much of today's curriculum is based on the left hemisphere the author is simply providing ideas on how to develop the right hemisphere and slowly move the learning process to the left hemisphere for better collaboration and then the students will learn to use both hemispheres and become full brained learners which ought to be the goal of teachers. The author also points out that only about 33% of students, as well as other people, are left hemisphere dominant and 67% are right hemisphere dominant. It has also been found that most ethnic minorities and women are right hemisphere dominant. Is it any wonder why the ethnic minorities and women do poorly in math and science? This also means that the standard school curriculum is based on 1/3 of the population. This why the author suggests the following techniques for teaching:

TEACHING TECHNIQUES FOR THE RIGHT HEMISPHERE TO ENHANCE LEFT HEMISPHIRIC FUNCTIONS OF "RIGHT BRAINERS"

ENRICHED ENVIRONMENTS FOR THE RIGHT (HEMISPHERE) BRAIN

When it comes to appreciating how the brain reacts to certain influences: start by removing threats from the learning environment. No matter how excited you are about adding positives to the environment, first work toward eliminating the negatives. These negatives include embarrassment, finger-pointing, unrealistic deadlines, forcing kids to stay after school, humiliation, sarcasm, isolation of students who wear attire of specific color. Teachers need to stop focusing on the stereotyping of students and begin to accept students because of their intelligence instead of the negative contents of the evening news and newspapers. These negatives prepare the ground for gang membership and school violence.

Once the threats are gone, teachers can go about the enrichment process because as they vary the type of environment the brain varies the way it develops. Teachers also need to ask Enrichment for whom? The myth for many years has been that only certain "gifted and talented" students would benefit from enrichment programs. Nothing could be further from the truth. Can we really afford to rob all of the "non gifted" students of their biological destiny to grow an enriched brain? If we do, we become recruiters for gangs, and unable to control violence in the schools. If students don't trust or have faith in the teachers how can teachers help students from school violence and gang membership?

ENRICHMENT THROUGH READING WRITING AND LANGUAGE

Schools should expose students to larger and more challenging vocabularies by age 12. Writing is one way to develop vocabulary. Usually the teachers teach kids printing before cursive writing. This makes little sense because the typical brain has not yet developed to make the fine visual-motor distinctions necessary. Kids will then have trouble with lower case Ds and Bs as well as H, N, A, and E. The frustration kids experience is for a good reason: Their brains are not ready for it. Cursive is much easier, and it's better to teach that first because with the advance of technology and computer keyboards, printing is less important than it was 50 years ago.

ENRICHMENT THROUGH THE ARTS

Recent brain research suggests that it's the arts that lay the foundation for later academic and career success. A strong arts foundation builds creativity, concentration, problem solving, self-efficacy, coordination, and self-discipline. The musical brain is persuasive because the brain may be designed for music, arts, and a music arts education has positive measurable and lasting academic and social benefits and should be required of all students. Moreover, music is a language that can enhance the abilities of kids who don't excel in the expression of verbal thinking. Consequently, as teachers we should increase the use of music in the classrooms. Some psychologists also suggest that playing Mozart quietly in the classroom enhances learning.

Teachers should remember that the days in which teachers could justify a classroom with one-way lectures are long gone. Today the evidence is overwhelming that enriched environments do develop a more intelligent brain. If children are to have the maximum opportunity to learn linear, sequential techniques it must be paired with approaches that enable students to see patterns, make use of visual and spatial thinking, and emphasize the WHOLE as well as the PARTS. Remember the movie, Renaissance Man, where Danny De Vito taught the students to be better soldiers by teaching them Shakespeare? The students in this class even developed a RAP song to Shakespeare's play to help them remember the characters and the play. At the end of the movie the soldiers volunteered to take a final exam because the teacher convinced them that they were smart. The soldiers completed the course and became better soldiers. If you have not seen the movies, please rent it and view it. However, the message is, if this teacher, played by Danny De Vito, could teach students to be better soldiers, why can't teachers teach students to be better citizens? Isn't it a sad commentary to say that during budget cuts, music and art are the first academic courses to be eliminated!

VISUAL THINKING

Balance verbal techniques with VISUAL strategies. Many ideas are better expressed and more easily understood using pictures, maps, diagrams, charts. Many people can not travel if they are told how to get from point A to point B because some students can't visualize the directions given, however, draw them a picture and they are on their way. This is called "mind maps." Use them as much as possible. They also offer students and teachers an additional way to express and explore ideas. In one experiment, kindergarten and primary students were taught kinetic molecular theory using pictures, concrete examples, and a single verbal text. They were introduced to the concepts of molecules in motion, states of matter, and changes in states of matter. The verbal abstractions were all represented graphically and with concrete examples familiar to the children. Two thirds of the students not only learned the concepts, but they remembered them a year later. This is impressive because these concepts were previously thought to be too complicated for children. Yet, as Albert Einstein once said, The words, or the language, as they are written and spoken, do not seem to play any role in the mechanism of thought..." Yet math and science teachers talk and talk and talk some more. Consequently, the author advocates that "hands on-minds on" strategies be the norm for teaching abstract subjects.

FANTASY

This is another form of visual thinking. As a teaching technique, it can be used to translate verbally presented material into images, making that information more accessible and comprehensible to students. It is also a way of giving students access to their rich store of RIGHT-HEMISPHERE images, and enhancing the quality of their creative work! Just remember that when students are looking out the window they are not inattentive. They are simply trying to form pictures by looking out the window and seeking real life things, such as trees or flowers. When teaching science, the author has the students pretend they are flying to the moon, with their eyes closed, and then describe what they felt. Some students have gotten airsick just by fantasizing they are flying in outer space. This fantasy is very realistic and the student's descriptions of what they learned were fantastic.

ELICIT LANGUAGE

Teachers cannot dismiss all verbal approaches when considering right hemisphere teaching. Objective language has as a goal the precision of meaning; it is the language of definition, which prizes clarity and abhors ambiguity. On the other hand evocative language is rich in associations, highly sensual and much less precise, it is more poetic. Think for a moment of lectures you have had. You will probably find that lecturers who made the deepest impression on you were those, which made effective use of evocative language. They were able to make a subject "COME ALIVE". Such people often have the ability to create an intense inner experience through their words. Teachers should know and use OBJECTIVE AND EVOCATIVE LANGUAGE.

METAPHORS

METAPHORIC or ANALOGIC thinking is the process of recognizing a connection between two seemingly unrelated things and it appears that these connections are probably made by the SILENT right hemisphere and transmitted to the left through some form of imagery. New learning does not occur in a vacuum; we learn something new by discovering how it relates to what we already know, and the clearer the connection, the easier and more thorough the learning. Metaphors---forge connections.

DIRECT EXPERIENCES

This is the utilization of Laboratory experiments, field trips including the use of manipulatives, simulations, and role-playing. The author often uses hands-on minds-on strategies and adheres to the ancient Chinese saying of, "tell me and I will forget, show me and I will remember, let me do it and I will learn."

MULTISENSORY LEARNING

Usage of tactile and kinesthetic movements, and let the children use as many of the five senses as possible when they are learning and remember, the more senses students use the more humanistic the lesson. However, the less senses used to learn the more abstract the lesson and the right brain will not be able to transfer abstract knowledge to the left brain.

MUSIC

Georgi Lozanov, a Bulgarian, uses music to facilitate and accelerate learning of foreign languages, and his techniques are being applied to other subjects as well. Is it any wonder why pre-school and kindergarten teachers use music so much when they teach. Why can't we use music in the higher grades? Maybe because we think that using music for teaching in the higher grades is too childish. What is wrong with being childish? Let us not forget that Picasso said that it took him a lifetime to learn how to paint like a child, which he thought was true art!

The thread that connects all techniques, are those that provide students with an alternative to the VERBAL, ANALYTICAL approach, which dominates so many classrooms. These techniques are not intended to replace traditional techniques; their purpose is to complement them so that the instructional program, like the integrated brain, can make use of a full range of skills and talents.

THE AUTHOR SUGGESTS THE FOLLOWING TEACHING METHODS FOR ALL STUDENTS AND ESPECIALLY GANG MEMBERS

The author teaches math and science methods to future teachers. However, he states that he does not teach math or science and that he teaches students a subject called math or science. Consequently, his focus is on the student and if the student does not understand the subject he then evaluates his delivery or strategy in teaching and changes his delivery or strategies until all students understand the subject. On the other hand, math and science teachers focus on the subject of math or science and if the students don't learn or understand the subject it is the students problem and the teachers seldom look at themselves to see if they are teaching the students. The author feels badly when such teachers brag that over 50% of their students failed math or science and his question is always, "what does this say about the teacher's teaching these subjects?" Consequently, the author makes the learning of math and science fun and exciting. How does he accomplish this? He use "hands-on minds-on" methods and includes the student's real life experiences. For instance: Children live with parallel lines long before they come to school. By the time lines are presented in GEOMETRY, the average student has seen thousands of examples in fences, windows, pictures, etc. Instead of referring to the parallel lines students have already experienced, most science teachers will draw parallel lines on the chalkboard and supply a definition. The students dutifully copy the new information into their notebook to be studied and remembered for the test that is sure to come. And the parallel lines suddenly become an abstract piece of information stored in the brain as a separate FACT.

Instead the author uses the student's experiences and builds on that knowledge, and as students learn the subject they form the correct definitions in their own words. In math the author teaches students to teach algebraic equations to fourth grade students by using bean sticks. However, he does not let them just manipulate the problems; he also stresses the proper terminology required in the specific math or science problem.

In science he does the same thing and the students learn biology, physics, and other scientific fields and they don't realize they are learning science. After they practice science experiments the students provide the definitions and terminology associated with each science field. In other words, he does not provide any definitions or terminology until the students learn and understand the science concept. If he didn't do this then the students would memorize instead of understanding the concepts of math and science.

In this chapter the author stresses the integration of all the subjects when teaching any subject and he presents, herein, a checklist that can be modified to use with any subject, but the example used is for math and science.

INTEGRATING MATH & SCIENCE INTO THE DAILY CURRICULUM

THE TASK:

It seems that this concept has reached a kindling point these days. It is actually a formula process and if the ideas are applied, as listed below, the teachers will find themselves teaching science and math with other subjects for the bulk of the day with little or no effort and the students may not even know that they are learning these abstract subjects. Teachers can take a single experiment, and built an entire curriculum around one idea. After the students get the hang of it they can start with any science or math concept.

Language Arts is used as an example, but the teacher can apply it to any subject matter.

1. Create vocabulary and spelling lists from the math or science unit.

2. Write a story about what it would be like to travel through a science concept or space.

3. Have the students create crossword puzzles, word scrambles, and word searches in math and science.

4. Write poems about the math or science concept.

5. Ask the students to make an oral report about math or science in class.

6. Create a continuation story with the kids adding one sentence to the story using ideas from the same unit.

7. Take the students on a mental field trip using ideas from the math or science unit (such as the fantasy trips)

8. Write a press release for a special discovery around the math or science concept.

9. Assign a written report for math or science.

INTEGRATING THE CURRICULUM WORKSHEET

The teacher may find this checklist helpful. Write the math or science concept that you wish to integrate at the top of the page and brainstorm.

The concept

_____

_____

_____

Art

_____

_____

_____

Language Arts

_____

_____

_____

P. E.

_____

_____

_____

Performing Arts

_____

_____

_____

Social Studies

_____

_____

_____

The Community

_____

_____

_____

SUMMARY OR CLOSURE

The author ends this chapter by stating that if teachers implement and administrators accept the ideas presented in this chapter the students may not have time, or the desire to join gangs, or to be violent. The author has found that the students enjoy themselves so much in what they are learning that gang leaders have very little opportunity, or success in recruiting new members. Because most students are accepted and taught in their learning style, the students to will be less inclined to think about school violence and gangs. There will always be those students that will get involved in negative activities, but teachers can diminish the negative activities a little at a time. Consequently, all that can be hoped for is that teachers save one student at a time. Realism dictates that we do no less and no more and if we save more than one student per day then teachers are then doing amazing things in the classroom.

PART II

REFERENCES TO BE USED TO BETTER DETECT GANG MEMBERSHIP

INTRODUCTION

It is not the purpose of this part of the book for readers to sit and memorize all this information. The purpose is for it to be used as a reference to be used when needed. For example, if a teacher or a parent sees the youngsters wearing a team cap for the Raiders, the reader then goes to the chapter addressing team hats and then the reader can find out what the hat means. However, the reader should not assume that just wearing a Raiders team hat that the youngster is a gang member. But if the hat is worn while the youngster is using gang language, and listening to RAP music that advocates violence, and further observations are conducted, then preventive measures should be implemented. The same is true for graffiti and tattoos. If two or more of these factors are associated with the youth then it should trigger more investigation that will lead to prevention.

The author suggests that this book and this section are readily available as a reference for further observations and implementation of preventive measures. The author realizes that this is almost a copy of what was said in the paragraph above, but it is repeated to emphasize that the reader does not have to learn or memorize the information. However, the information in this section is a valuable resource to help deter gang activity in the home, school, and the community.

CHAPTER 8

THE GANG LANGUAGE

INTRODUCTION

Much of this list comes from: Lewis & Associates chapter 17 pages 1-27. However, It also comes from the author's personal experiences and the Internet. The following terms or vocabulary list can be vital to all those agencies and people concerned with the gang culture and prevention. It is by understanding some of these terms or words that society can identify possible wanna bee, or gang members. However, it must be remembered that like any language these words are always in transition. Especially, when gang members learn that others understand their slang, terms, or words they will change them. Everyone who is involved in prevention of gang activities can benefit from this chapter, but please use them with care. The author's suggestion for using this chapter is use the word lists when teachers or parents hear unfamiliar words or sayings. Write the words on a piece of paper then try to find them on these lists and then find what they mean after school or at home..

Following are two examples on how these terms can be beneficial to educators and parents:

1. When students are heard using some of the terms, more than once, the teachers and others can begin preventive measures and this does not mean "disciplinary" measures. Keep it in mind that the purpose of any knowledge is to diagnosis, prevent and help students from becoming wannabes or gang members.
2. If parents understand these terms then they can also begin preventive

measures at home. If these terms are constantly used, the parents can visit their children's bedroom and see if there are any of these words on walls, backpacks, or other locations, and looking for other signs showing gang activity.

Note: other signs of gang activity are listed in other chapters, but as a quick reference these are other signs of gang activity: Remember that if the color red or blue is worn daily and on everything, if gang hand signs are used by youngsters, or their actions or friends change for no apparent reason, they are indicators of gang activity. This is the time to take corrective and positive measures. One clear sign is when Latino or Asians youngsters begin to lose respect for their parents. The list can go on, but the message is clear. Moreover, some of the terms used are historical and come from other eras and were familiar and used by the author. In other words the Spanish part of the list "may be recycled words used since the 1940s."

A VOCABULARY LIST

VOCABULARY	**THE MEANING/S**
How Numbers Are Used:	
1/2 of tree	1/2 of drugs (1/2 oz, lb, etc.) Marijuana
1/8 of greens	1/8 of drugs usually 1/8 oz. of marijuana
13	Means mafia-eme-la eme- Sureños
14	Means la familia-Norteños,
20 cents	$20 worth of cocaine
8 track	2 1/2 grams of cocaine
9 mike	9 mm handguns

VOCABULARY

Words Used:

THE MEANING/S

A

A — Acid, LSD, hallucination drug

Are you on? — Do you have drugs for sale?

Are you looking? — Do you want drugs?

abusado — alert

ace kool — best friend, backup

aci — heroin

aguitado — mad/furious

aguja — needle

ain't no thang — no problem, nothing to it, simple

al alba con los perros — lookout for the cops

al vato lo chingaron — they beat him/screwed/fucked him

al rato — later

armas — arms, weapons

amber alert — keep eyes and ears open

aztlan — former Mexican territories of the southwest

B

Bass head — Some one that smokes Crack Cocaine

Bump — A line of cocaine, usually snorted through the nose.

Baller/balling — gang member making money (high roller)

Barrio — neighborhood

Betty — attractive female syn: Fly, freak, mama, hoe

BGD — Black gangster disciples, Chicago folk

VOCABULARY	**THE MEANING/S**
Blancas/blancos	Whites, males and females
Blob	term used by Crips for blood gang members
Blondie	bonds
Blood	non-crip gang member
Blue	color that crips identify with
Bo	marijuana
Bod out	under influence of marijuana
Boned out	quit/chicken out/left/backed down
Book	run, get away, leave
Borrego	small bag
Bote	jail
Break down	shotgun
Break	run, get away
Bucket	old, regged car
Bud	marijuana
Bullet	one year in custody
Bumper kit	girls butt
Bumping titties	fighting
Burn	to beat the competition
Burnt	something which no longer can be used
Busted	shot at someone
	Buster young guy trying to be a gang member, or one who doesn't yet live up to gang standards
Busting	shoot at someone

C

C	well seasoned-educated hermano (brother)

VOCABULARY	THE MEANING/S
C/	Carnal/NF member/Familiano
Cabollar	to rap
Caca	drugs, shit
Calmate culo	calm down asshole
Camarada	friend
Canton	house
Carcancha	car/junker
Carcel	jail
Carga	heroin
Carnal	brother
Carnala	sister
Carrucha	car
Chale	hell no
Chansa	chance
Chante	house/home
Chavala	girl/little girl
Check it out	listen to what I have to say
Cheese out	give up/snitch
Chicanismo	state of chicano brotherhood
Chicanos no se rajan	Chicanos have courage, never give up
Chill out	stop it/don't do that/calm down
Chillin	hanging out
Chingasos	fighting
Chrisy	Slang word for meth.
Chiva	heroin/cocaine
Cholo	Mexican gang member, but historically it meant some one looked and talked differently
Chota	police

VOCABULARY	THE MEANING/S
Chuco	veteranos, veteran of a gangs-pachuco (Zuit Zooter) of the old days
chuntaro/mojados	referring Mexican nationals in the US
chupar	to smoke. to suck, to cook to brown
clavo	needle
cluck	a chicken, or a person that is not reliable, or some one that smokes crack cocaine.
colors	bandanas, or articles meaning gang affiliation
colum or commercial	Colombian marijuana
como son pinchis	what bastards/ chicken-shit dudes
compa	compadre-friend
compas	godparents
comps	godfather
con safos C/S	same back to you (Latino graffiti symbol)
con	with
concentrada	hashish
concha	gossiper
controlamos	we control
courting in	Initiation into gang
courting out	expulsion from a gang
crab	blood nick name for "crip" member
crack	rock cocaine
crib	house/home
Crip	certain Black street gang members
Cuca	the barrio of Cucamonga
Cuete	gun
Cuz	what Crips call each other
Cuzz	Crip

VOCABULARY	THE MEANING/S

D

Daddy mac	attractive male syn: mac daddy, freak daddy
Dead rag	red rag
Dedo	to finger someone
Destinations	the front of the bus
Duce & a half	.25 auto
Dis	no respect/disrespect
Disciples	a folk gang from Chicago (B.G.D.)
Dissed	given disrespect/disrespect
Dissin	no disrespect/disrespect
Do a ghost	to leave/leave the scene
Doing a Rambo	attack a person (armed)
Doin a jack	committing a robbery
Do you Bang?	Are you a gang member?
Double deuce	.22 caliber gun
Down for mine	ability to protect self
Down	in, & part of the group or action
DR	daily report
Drag	ability to sweet talk girls
Draped	person wearing a lot of gold jewelry
Dub	A $20.oo bag of weed (marijuana), or a double up on cocaine ($20 will make you $40,. Etc.
Dump in	shooting a gun
Dumped on	Got shot
Dura	hashish
Durag	handkerchief wrapped around head
Dusted	under the influence of PCP

VOCABULARY	**THE MEANING/S**
	E
Eastly	very ugly person
Eight track	2 1/2 grams of cocaine
Eight ball	Bag of cocaine
El barrio	the neighborhood
El condado	the county jail
Ericket	term for east coast Crip
ese	term for Mexican gang member
ese vato	hey dude, hey man
esseys	Mexicans
everything is everything	it's all right
	F
Fa chezzy	for the love of money
fade	to blend colors
Familia	family
Fatty	A line of meth.
familiano	nuestra familia member (Norteños)
federatin of barrios	Chicano gangs in LA areas
feria	money
fifty	police/comes for TV series Hawaii five-O
fila	knife
filero	knife
filters	information/data
firing on someone	throwing a punch/shooting at someone
firme	good/straight person
five-o	police, syn: one time

VOCABULARY	THE MEANING/S
flaco	used to describe a thin subject
flojo	lazy
flue rag	blue rag-bandana worn by crips.
folk	an affiliation of Chicago gangs
folks	gang nation in mid-west (Chicago based)
four-five	.45 caliber gun
frajos	cigarettes
freak	good looking girl
fred	unattractive, unintelligent male syn: barney
fresh	good looking, clean
frying	some one on acid, LSD
frog	jumps in anybody's car or girl with really low moral standards.
full 60	Priority alert, weapon out, riot coming down, shot might be fired

G

G. P.	General Principle
gaffing	stealing, same as racking
gaffle up	to confuse, mess up, hurt
gang banger	gang member
gang banging	general gang activity
ganga	gang
gank	to steal or imitation rock cocaine
gat	handgun
gavachos	white boys or Anglos
geek	someone who is loaded, high, strange, or abnormal
get down	fight

VOCABULARY	THE MEANING/S
GF	ghetto or familiano (ghetto -warrior)
Gig	gathering, party
Glass	slang word for Meth.
Grifa	marijuana
Grills	the back of the bus
Grind	Some one that's out selling drugs all night.

H

HB	home base
Hard	Crack Cocaine or some thing that's strong.
Half	half oz., lb., etc of drugs
He's from nowhere	any gang member
Head up	fight someone
Head hunter	female who does sexual acts for cocaine
Here	bag of marijuana
HHRs	house hold rules
High rollin	making good money, drug dealing
Hoe	a girl that has sex with a lot of different guys.
Holding down	controlling turf or area
Home boy or Homey	fellow gang member
Homie	one of the boys from the neighborhood
Homies	boys from the neighborhood
Hoo-rah	loud talking
Hood	neighborhood
Hook	phoney, imitation
Hoopty	car

VOCABULARY	THE MEANING/S
Horale (orale)	alright, acknowledgment
House name	nickname, a houser is given
Houser	people who go into parties held at home
Hueros	Anglos
Huevon	lazy
Huevos	having a lot of balls, guts
Hustler	not into gangs, only out make money

I

Irma	information

J

Jack in/jacked	robbing or stealing
Jacked up	beat up, assaulted
Jaina	girlfriend
Jam	song, music, also leave quickly
Jammed	confronted
Jefa/jefe	mother, father, mother, boss
Jefito (a)	mother, boss, father
Jim jones	marijuana joint laced with cocaine, PCP dripped
Jiving	attempting to fool someone
Joto	fag/gay
Jump in jumped on	initiate into a gang, usually in a fight
Jura	police

K

K. B's	Form of marijuana
K9	law enforcement officer

VOCABULARY	**THE MEANING/S**
Keyed	some one high on marijuana
Kibbles and bits	crumbs of cocaine
Kick it	to relax, to chill out
Kicking it	relaxing with fellow gang member
Kicking back	relaxing, killing time
King	the best with the most
Knockout	loser of battle, give up crew name
Kool	it's all right

L

L	A loss or life sentence
La causa	the cause
La trola	the match
La raza	the race
La raza unida	the united race
La placa	shield, slang for police
La movida	Illegal activity
La ley	cops, pigs, fuzz
La chinga	the damn activity (the job)
La jura	the police
El jale	the job
La migra	border patrol
Lady	girlfriend
Lambion	kiss ass
Land marks	fixed street objects (signs, poles, curbs)
Lets bail	lets leave
Lets ride on someone	seek someone out, usually means retaliation
Liquid juice	P. C. P.

VOCABULARY	THE MEANING/S
Lit up	shot at
Lizard butt	ugly girl
Loc's	dark sunglasses
Loc-ed	acting crazy
Loco	crazy
Los pinches placas	the fuckin pigs, cops, fuzz

M

Main man	best friend/backup
Maricon	homosexual, or gay
Mark	want-to-be gang member
Marrano	pig, police
Mayate, tinto	Black person
Chanate	home
Mecha	match or student org.
Menso/a	idiot
Mos	mojado, Mexican nationals, undocumented
Mobile	proper, nice looking
Molded/scratch	embarrassed
Mosca	pest/fly
Mota	hashish/marijuana
Mud duck	ugly girl

N

N/A	new arrival
Nada	nothing
Nel	no
Nick	to steal, same as racking/$5.00 of marijuana

VOCABULARY	**THE MEANING/S**
Nine mike	9mm handgun
No copees	don't cop out
NRT	maestro-nuestra raza, teacher
Nut up	angry-mad at somebody

O

O	organization
O. C.	Out of control
O/G	original gangster
OAS	over all security
Off the hook/chain	some thing that's cool, or some one that's crazy
On hit	good, exciting, syn: cool, funky, dope, kickin
On the pipe	free basing cocaine
On point	just right
One time	one police officer approaching
Onta	Ontario California barrio
Orale	okay, right, or stop fooling around

P

Packing	gang member has gun in possession
Par lay	hanging out
Pay back	vendetta/retaliation for a wrong
Paz	peace
Pedo	drunk or bullshit
Pelon	bald
Pendejo	stupid
People	a gang nation in Chicago/rival or folk
Perros	slang for cops (means dogs)

VOCABULARY	THE MEANING/S
Pezzy	pound of drugs
Philly	cigar wrap used for marijuana
Piece	firearm
Pill	to kill someone, syn: smoke
Pinchis	bastards, chicken shit dudes
Pinta	penitentiary, prison, county jail
Pinto	state prisoner, ex con
Pipirin	food
Pistiar	to drink alcohol
Pisto	booze, an alcoholic drink
Pistiar	to drink booze
Plata	outfit/money
Playboy	weapon
Player	promiscuous person
Ponte trucha	watch out, get with it, look out
Popped a cap	shot at someone
Por vida	for life
Primo	marijuana joint laced with cocaine (actually means cousin)
Pugging	fighting
Pulling you on	making a fool of you
Puntas	needle
Pura caca/pedo	pure bullshit or fart
Puto snizzle	snitch informant
Puto	whore or gay male

Q

Q. T. pie	1/4 lb. Of drugs
Que paso?	what happened?

VOCABULARY	THE MEANING/S
Que gacho	bummer, bad scene, bad experience
Quete	gun

R

RA	raza administrations
Rack	to steal
Racking	stealing clothing, paint, etc
Rag	color of gang, handkerchief
Raise	leave
Rajar	to open up, squeal
Rambo gauge	sawed off shotgun
Ramfla	car
Rank	status within gang
Rank on	bring disrespect to themselves or the crew
Rank out	failed to claim a crew or back up crew members
Rata	rat, snitch
Raton	label for informer, snitch, or rat
Recruiting	looking for good looking girls
Red eye	hard stare
Red	color that blood gang identifies with
Red alert	serious/potential threat on the yard or in the unit, team up, no games, ready to defend self
Refin	food
Refinar	to eat
REG	regiment
Relaje	snitch, turncoat
Ride on	go to rival neighborhood & attack gangs

VOCABULARY	THE MEANING/S
Ride	car
Rifa	marijuana
Rifa, rifan	rule
Rifamos	we rule
Rock	crystallized cocaine
Rock	rock cocaine
Rock house	a house where rock cocaine is sold
Rode on	went hunting for rival gang member
Rolled up	arrested
Rollin	doing well, have a nice car
Roo-rah	loud talking
Rooster	piru member
Roscoe	Black gang slang for a gun, or small handgun, Saturday night special
RSD	raza security department
Ru	piru member
Ruca (o)	old woman, wife (old man, husband) old lady, young chick
Ruff neck	some one that's hard core (will do anything)
Rush	ability to sweet talk girls
Rushed	attack

S

Sabes que ese	you know what man?
Sacate	grass, marijuana
Sancho	wife's boyfriend
Scandalous	dead beat person, bad person
Siempre	forever
Set	neighborhood

VOCABULARY	THE MEANING/S
Sherm	PCP
Shermed	high on PCP
Shiri	secure
Shirley	security
Shooter	gang member that uses firearms
Simon	yes, ok man
Skeezer	ugly girl
Slanging	selling cocaine on the street
Sling/slang	deal or sell coke
Slob	Crip name for blood member
SM	squad member, foot soldier
Smoked	some one that got killed
Smoked out	addiction, cocaine user, weak
Smoker	person who smokes cocaine
Snaps	money
Soft	powder cocaine or some thing that's weak
Soldado	gang soldier
Soup coolers	big lips
Spot	a store to shoplift from
Sprung	a person addicted to cocaine
Squab	fight, argue
Sriw	super race is white
Stall it out	stop doing what you are doing
Strawberry	female who does sexual acts for cocaine
Surfer	white person involved in gang activity
Swag	cheap for marijuana
Sweated	questioned by police

VOCABULARY	**THE MEANING/S**
Syndicate	group of associates or friends, syn: posse, houser

T

Talco	cocaine, powder
Talking head	argue, wanting to fight
Talking smack	aggressive talking
Tanque	jail
To the curb	bad position to be in, or doesn't belong, non-conformist
The whole thing	a pound of weed/marijuana, or a kilo of cocaine
Tight	some thing that looks good
Tonia	weapon
Tonto	fool, dumb
Torcido	twisted, to be arrested, busted
Torcido por nada	busted for nothing
Total	all the way
Tray eight	.38 caliber gun
Trick	phony, sissy, or a girl that performs sex acts for money, or a male that loves prostitutes
Trip	too much, something else
Turkish	heavy ornament gold necklace, earrings
Tweeker	some one that uses meth or crack cocaine
Twenty cents	$20 worth of cocaine

U

UBN	United Blood Nation

VOCABULARY	THE MEANING/S
Una chinga	a lot
Up on it	successful drug dealer. Also in the know on the drug scene

V

Varrio	neighborhood
Vato	guy
Vato loco	crazy guy, or gang member
Vendidos	one who has sold out, turncoat
Veterano	excon, or old guy who has been around
Vice lords	a Chicago gang, they are rivals of folks
Vick	to steal, syn: rack, go on a beer or candy run
Vida loca	crazy life
Viva	long live

W

Wacha	to dig (seen on tattoos)
Water	PCP
Wave	short, close-cropped hair
What hood you from?	What's the name of your gang?
What's it hitting for	how much do you want for it $$$?
What it "b" like	blood greeting
What it "c" like	crip greeting
What set you from	asking what gang you're from?
What's the word	what do you want to do?
What's cracking?	What are you doing?
What's up	what's going on?

VOCABULARY	THE MEANING/S
Where you from	asking someone if they're from any gang
Wilma	unattractive female
Word	okay, alright
WPNs	weapons

X

X	ecstasy

Y

Y/P	yard patrol
Ya estuvo	it's over with
Yaw baste	enough
Yucca	marijuana
Yierba/zacate	marijuana, herb, grass

Black, Asian, or Latino gang members can use the words, listed above,, but the author feels that this list is especially valuable for the Asian and Spanish bilingual teachers, and other teachers who have not been exposed to some of the African American and other words listed. However, remember that slang terms used by youngsters change all the time, but if you pay attention to the youth of today you can notice the changes taking place. Teachers, parents and other adults must keep their eyes and ears open to what the youth are saying in order to penetrate the youth's thinking, or feelings on a daily basis.

CHAPTER 9

RAP MUSIC AS USED BY GANGS

INTRODUCTION

The author has included the following information separately so that the reading of the book will be less cumbersome instead of including it in the other chapters of this book it is here. The information on RAP music is in this chapter. Like everything related to gangs, RAP music changes. However, this chapter presents ideas on how RAP reinforces and condones gang violence

This information could be valuable to parents, school administrators, school boards, and teachers and other agencies if they want to address the real problem of gangs and school violence. The author offers ideas and suggestions, but will the information prevent gangs in the schools and community? No, unless the book is read in its entirety, and if the ideas presented in the book are implemented. After reading this book will it help prevent gangs in the classroom? It could! Will the book stop gangs in the classroom? No, but it may decrease gang membership and activity and with care and time it could prevent the killing of young people.

It must be remembered that if we save the life of one youngster, and if we work on this effort one day at a time and one youngster at a time we could decrease gang violence in the classroom in the next few years. Thus far the efforts of many community agencies have made many attempt to prevent gangs. However, we need to make this effort a community effort and work as a team rather than become territorial between each agency. The lives and survival of the young people and the total community is at stake, therefore, all efforts and agencies are equally important and can be effective.

RAP music is extensive and there is not enough space in this book to include all of it. But there are about 15 pages related to just RAP music. Consequently, the author further recommends that the readers log on to web sites that contain more information about RAP. The author will include RAP music as used by Latino, Asian and African American gang structures. Because Latino RAP or music is not very extensive it will be the starting point for presenting this information.

CHICANO MUSIC/RAP: AND IT'S INFLUENCE ON GANG VIOLENCE AND CULTURE

By Gabe Morales

According to Gabe Morales much of the media focus has been on black rap artists. But music has played an historical role relative to Latino gangs. Popular Latino music artists have been influenced by the gang culture, as well. Oldies and Rap continue to be popular with Latino gang members of this decade.

The influence of Latino gangs upon music, and vice versa, goes back to the so-called "Bandido" days of the 1800s. Corrido songs were written about the exploits of Mexican rebel leaders and what many sympathizers felt was "gringo oppression" during the Mexican-American War. Songs or corridos became even more popular during the Mexican Revolution of 1910. During the revolution, the rebels sang a popular song named "La Cucaracha" (The cockroach). The song has a line that says, "La cucaracha la cucaracha ya no quiere caminar, porque le falta, por que necesita, mariguana que fumar." (The cockroach doesn't want to walk anymore because it doesn't have and it needs marijuana to smoke). Ironically this song is often sung in schools and by young children, but of course marijuana is left out and another word is used.

In the Pachuco or Zoot Suit days, big band songs, of the 1940s and 50s were based upon the 1940s Zoot Suit Riots in L.A. and other major cities. Chuck Higgins, who grew up in the Mexican Aliso Village barrio, released "The Pachuko Hop." Based on the success of that song, Higgins released another song, Wetback Hop. This title would undoubtedly cause quite a commotion nowadays, but not in those days. "Chico Sesma" promoted L.A.-area concerts and had a radio program that was popular with Chicano youth in the 1950s and gang members. In particular, the Chicanos in this era loved ballads sung by black artists by the so-called "Doo Wop" groups.

Ricardo Valenzuela from Pacoima, California, who was better known as Richie Valens, was just one of the many popular Latino singers in southern California who played at concerts in El Monte's Legion Stadium, the Pomona Auditorium, and other music halls. Art Leboe, a popular disc jockey, played many of these songs on his "Oldies, but Goodies" compilations.

Dick Hugg, better known as "Huggy Boy." was another popular disc jockey during this time period. Today, gang members listen to similar radio shows such as "The Sancho Show" in Southern California and the "Bajito Onda Show" in northern California. The song "Louie, Louie," still a popular favorite at Mexican-American for its Latino beat, was the subject of an FBI investigation (one of Edgar J. Hoover's many paranoid delusions), and was almost banned by right-wing politicians because it had a mix of white, black, and Chicano music and rebellious a message.

Louie, Louie was a party rebel song enjoyed by Chicanos and American kids alike. A great explanation of this song is now given at the new Experience Music Project Museum built by one-time rebel (and now an established billionaire) Paul Alien. The Kingmen, who recorded Louie, Louie, were a Seattle-based band from the 1960s. The song remains popular with many of today's youth.

During the 1960s and early 1970s, an East L.A. band, "The Midnighters," produced a song in Whittier Boulevard, named after a famous "Lowrider cruising strip" and culminated their career with a song entitled Chicano Power, about the east L.A. riots in the 1960s. This song was very popular with members of the "Brown Berets" and Chicano gang members, who were sometimes called "Batos Locos" according to David Reyes, a Chicano music historian. A band called "El Chicano" wrote a Latin jazz tune called "Viva Tirada" (which roughly translates to "long live throwing down," a reference to getting into the party groove). The term "throwing down" is now a reference to throwing down gang and the finger signs used in today's street gang culture. Kid Frost later sampled this song in his song, this is for "La Raza," which was heavily gang-influenced. The video for the song prominently depicts Cholo-style gangsters.

There are other popular songs that are gang-influenced or have been adopted by gangs as their theme songs. I'm "Eighteen with a Bullet," recorded by Pete Wingfield, was included in a 1970's Chicano low-rider music album. Eastside Story, Volume 12, is the 18th Street Gang's theme song. Slippin' into Darkness, by WAR, is popular amongst tecatos (junkies). The Pirus adopted "Natural High" by Bloodstone, a Black gang at Folsom Prison adopted the song as their theme song.

While these songs are popular with non-gang members, there are some music groups who are increasingly involved in hard-core promotion of gang warfare and violence towards law enforcement officers. When the Hip-Hop culture first began to gain momentum in the late 1970s, Latinos were very active as DJ's, break-dancers, and taggers, but few got on the microphone to rap. However, this has changed and many Latino rappers are now "getting on the mic." The Hip-Hoppers call this "spittin'," and popular rappers like Eminem may make references like, "just wanna' spit it, get wit it..." Some of the present-day Latino gangsta' rappers make Kid Frosfs, "La Raza" look like a church hymn.

Norteño Gang Specialist Jared Lewis, of the Modesto, California, Police Department, and Deputy Fernando Velasco, of the San Francisco County Sheriffs Office, have pointed to a trend of Norteños gangs rallying around Latino rap music companies to get their messages out to young people in a popular music format. The Generation of United Norteños (GUN) Coalition has recorded music promoting the gang life-style, as has Black-n-Brown productions in the Bay area. The Darkroom Familia (Salinas and Tracy California area) has also released a recent CD entitled Gang Stories. The CD liner notes from Gang Stories state:

"The authorities pulled the CD off store shelves but because we're not just rappers, we just live la vida loca." "Violence solves everything!" The cops are trying to pick us all off, this is Darkroom Familia, Homeboy, till the wheels fall off! - Sir Dyno." symbols which have become entrenched within the Hispanic street gang culture often originated within the music scene. One of these is the "Smile Now. Cry Later." Happy Face/Sad Face tattoos worn by many gang members to signify smile now cry later.

According to the information that has been gathered, a 1960's song by Sonny (Ozuna) and the Sunliners called "Smile Now (for My Friends) and Cry Later" appeared as a reproduction on the East Side Story low rider records (now in reprint) that were popular in the seventies.

For Chicano gang members, the phrase "Smile Now, Cry Later" also represents Mi Vida Loca (translated as "My Crazy Life"). The term Smile Now is symbolic of the gangster lifestyle of running the streets and partying with friends and "homies." But, the life style leads ultimately to getting busted, going to jail or prison, and being away from loved ones, thus "Cry Later." Los Solidos, a gang in the northeastern US., also uses this phrase as a symbol of their gang, and is also commonly used by non-Chicano gang members around the US.

However, this phrase is not a reference to any specific gang, but is more of a commentary on gang life in general. Al Valdez, an Investigator with the Orange County, California, District Attorney's Office, notes: "The phrase, 'smile now cry later,' has to do with the craziness of gang life. Play now and pay later. It is a generic gang tattoo, and not gang specific, but having it alone may not mean the wearer is a gangster by court "standards." More recently, Kid Frost made a 1995 rap-release of the song "Smile Now Die Later" and young people across the US. has adopted the phrase to fit the "live fast, die young" mentality of the street. It might be very easy to conclude that much of this ethnic music is gang related, however, that conclusion is not warranted.

These types of music, including Oldies, are popular with a wide segment of the overall population. However, the gang lifestyle has influenced the songs of many Latino singers and bands, which grew up in gang-infested neighborhoods. This music, in turn, may influence the behavior of the younger gang member/listener but is not necessarily indicative of gang involvement.

At this point in time, Latino RAP has had a relatively small market share when compared to other forms of rap especially by African Americans. With the increasing numbers of Latino youth in the United States and the crossover with the "Latino Hit Explosion" of 1999, this style of music may eventually increase in popularity. Professionals working with gang members should be aware of the role music has historically played in the gang culture, as well as the increasing use of music by gangs to increase recruitment and support for their gang life style. The growing violence in the lyrics in these songs also seems to indicate a trend toward willingness on the part of gang members to commit violent acts directed at law enforcement officers.

The RAP sang by Latinos and Blacks is often used to send messages to the masses of young listeners who often hear the RAP music that they love. However, much of that type of music preaches violence, rape, killing law enforcement personnel, non safe sex and many other messages that the youth need not hear. How can we stop all this? The author doesn't know, but if adults listen to it they will learn much about how the young are motivated toward unacceptable behavior. However, there is guarantee of "freedom of speech" and these songs are protected under this constitutional amendment. Here's a thought, what would happen if most adults told their children that they love RAP? If adults fake it the young would probably say, "if adults like this music maybe it is not so cool" and quite listening to it.

AFRICAN AMERICAN RAP: AND INFLUENCE ON GANG VIOLENCE AND CULTURE

African American RAP is very similar to the Mexican RAP music and it is included here and some of the information has been extracted from the WWW and accessible at: HYPERLINK http://www.rapdict.org. http://www.rapdict.org, or rec.music.hip-hop.

The Rap vocabulary is listed below and it is not intended to show the only correct spelling of words; slang is mostly a spoken language and no one knows how to spell it in exact English language. A word might mean something someone and not to others, or to the reader because all words and corresponding meanings have been put in the list and remains on the list until challenged by gang members. The author has not followed English rules and writing out words fully or correctly. Most verbs are usually written differently, though; for example the word "cruising" which will may be spelled like "cruising," or brother is often written as "brotha." Some words starting with an "f" letter may often be written as "ph", like phat or phunky. And what do we think of a word like Doowutchalike? Where possible the author has added a source to show in what context the word is being used. The author does not take credit for the vocabulary list because the credit goes to the Internet web sites and other authors.

A VOCABULARY LIST

The following word "dap" is shown to denote how the vocabulary list was formed and used. The letter "n" means noun and the "v" means a verb. Therefore:

dap   1) (n) Sort of high-five type of handshake. "Gimme a dap, I'll give you one back" Ice T. (Ziplock [1991])

                2) (n) Dignity and Pride, old slang (think 70s here).

Note the "a source" as in "just any source," the author doesn't mean "the source" because that would take ages of debating. Also note that in slang or dialects the grammar is not strongly typed, so nouns can be verbs etc. Slang for gun and penis is almost always interchangeable. Please help making this list more complete. If it was not for the help of the "UseNet alt. rap community" this list wouldn't have been listed

The following list contains just a few examples of RAP music and is intended as a preview of RAP music concerning the gang culture. For further information log onto the web sites listed in this chapter. Furthermore, the author also believes that these few examples could drive an English teacher a little crazy. Legend (n) means noun and (v) means verb

The word used	**It's meaning**
lac	(n) Short for Cadillac. Macks drive" lacs Big Mello [1993].
1 and 2	(n) Turntables. "DJ behind the 1 and 2."
1-2 checker	1)(n) Checking the MIC. 2) (n) Checking the scene.
10	See Mac 10. "Had my ten in my hand" ---Coolio Gangsta's [1995]).
10%	(n) See 5%. "Ten percent took a loss" Boots of The Coup."
107.5 Big	(n) The big "urban format" station in Chicago, Illinois. 107.5 WGCI, home of the nationally syndicated "Tom Joyner Morning Show," a focal point for activism and unity in the black community.

The word used	It's meaning
1200	1) (n) The Technics SL 1200 is regarded as the best turntable for DJing. The reason for this is its very, very high torque. If you hit the start/stop button, the platter will reach top speed within a 1/4th revolution. Not many turntables can match that. "My DJ you know 1200's he's using," don't!" Schoolly, D. (I don't like rock en roll [??]) 2) (n) SP-1200 sampler, a top of the line product.
1555	The year the first slave-ships arrived in America. "Sayin" 1555 how "ím livin" Public Enemy (Can't truss it [??]).
186	(n) Police term for a murder or homicide. To be on the lookout for someone who is trying to kill you.
187	(n) Californian penal code number for homicide. The police in California use the penal code numbers as shorthand on the radio. For example in Oregon the code for homicide is 163.0051, which is different from California. "Try to set me up for a 21", fuck around and get caught up in a 187 Dr. Dre (Let me ride [1992]).
2 to 4	(n) The duration of an imprisonment sentence, two to four years in jail. "Hit with a 2 to 4 is difficult" - Mobb Deep (Survival of the fittest [1995]).

The word used	**It's meaning**
20	1) (n) See twenty sack. "'I'm an addict for sneakers, 20 of buddah and bitches with beepers" NAS (New York state of soft mind [1994]). 2) (n) 20-inch rims on car wheels. <EM> "Twenties, TVs, leather and wood" </EM> Lil Bow Wow (Bounce with me [2000]).
21 & Lewis	(n) Street-corner in Long Beach, California. "I hung a left at two-one and Lewis" -Warren G. (Regulate [1994]).
21 Cerritos	(n) Long Beach crip set. The Dogg Pound and Warren G have rumored association with them. "But you don't really know about, you know, the Cerritos silly ho" Daz (Who gotz some gangsta shit [1994]).
211	(n) Police code for armed robbery. "Try to set me up for a 211, fuck around and get caught up in a 187" Dr. Dre (Let me ride [1992]).
212	(n) A New York area code.

The word used	**It's meaning**
213	1) (n) the name of a group with Snoop, Nate Dogg and Warren, G. This group was separated when they all got big. "Way back then 213 was the clique" Warren G (Do you see [1994]). 2) (n) Also, 213 was the area code for Long Beach before it got 310, which now is the area code for a large portion of southern California, including Compton. Inglewood is 213 nowadays. 3) (n) 213 was named after a car (not a motor vehicle but an alliance of inmates in a prison). See Ice-Tís book "Who gives a Fuck?" for reference. There are other cars as well but most West coast and/or Death Row rappers claim to be affiliated with the 213 car (not to be confused with the set somebody claims)
22	(n) 22-caliber gun. "Twenty-two automatic on my person" Beastie Boys (Posse in Effect [1986]) Police code for drugs. 24/7, 24/7/36
226	(n) Police code for drugs.
24/7, 24/7/365	(n) All the time, from 24 hours a day, 7 days a week, 365 days a year.
25 with an L	(n) 25 years to life sentence. 25 with an "z" - Snoop Doggy Dog (Murder was the case [1993]).
30	(n) A firearm of .30 caliber.
310	(n) the area code for Long Beach.

The word used	**It's meaning**
313	(n) 313 is the phone area code for Detroit, Michigan, home of Eminem. "And these brothers representing the 313" - Eminem (Infinite LP [1996])
357	(n) A .357 Magnum pistol. "357 break it on down LL Cool J." .357 Break it on down [1987]).
36 chambers	1) (n) The 36 chambers a warrior has to go through to become a Shaolin. Every chamber has a special task the warrior has to complete in order to be able to continue to the next chamber. The RZA said in an interview with Billboard Magazine that there are nine members in the Clan, and each member has four chambers in his heart, which makes 9x4 = 36 chambers. 2) (n) there are 36 "death-points" on the body, each separated from the other at 10-degree intervals, where the trained Wu expert can cause death at a single blow.
38	1 (n) 38 caliber pistol. 2) (n) "38 hot" means very angry.
380	(n) A 380 caliber handgun. Unpacked and I grabbed my three eighty cause where we stay'n niggaz look shady" Ice Cube (Summer Vacation [1991]).
4 pound	(n) 45 caliber (1 caliber = 1/100th inch) gun.
4-5-6	(n) See celo. See the song 456 by Kool G Rap.

The word used	It's meaning
4-9-3-11	n) the numbers represent letters of the alphabet; 4 is D, 9 is I, and so on. These numbers spell "dick." I be "comin through like the 4-9-3-11 tearing up the power-U" Method Man (Meth vs. Chef [1994]).
40	1(n) A 40-ounce bottle of malt liquor. "Use to drink every day, straight 40's to the head" -Ice-T. (Ed [1991]). 2) n) A 40 caliber gun "With my 40 and my 40 to the fucking dome."
411	(n) Information, from the US phone number for information.
4:20	(n) the time to smoke some marijuana. 1)
50	1) (n) A police officer, from the series Hawaii Five-0. The word is used mainly in East LA. "Five-0 said freeze and I got numb" Public Enemy (Bring the Noise). 2) (n) A 5.0 liter Ford Mustang, which is used as a police vehicle in some areas.
5 on it	(n) Five dollars on a sac of marijuana. "I got five on it" - The Luniz (I got five on it (1995)

The word used	**It's meaning**
% Nation	(n) A group which started as an offshoot of the NoI. They teach that any large group of people, and more specifically, the African American nation, can be divided into three groups, the 85% = basically the ignorant masses which need to be led, the 5% = the people with true knowledge of self whose job it is to lead the masses and fight against the 10%, the 10% = people who have partial knowledge of self and use it to gain power and wealth by exploiting the 85, also referred to as "bloodsuckers of the poor." The chosen percentages are what they feel that the percentages are within the black community. These numbers are neither universal (all though these groups do exist within any large group) nor unchangeable. "That'll be the day the five percent eat swine - Dred Scott (Breakin" combs [1994]).
5 plated	adj.) Nickel plated.
5000	(interj) a farewell bidding, from "I'm outta here" which evolved to "I'm Audi" and to 5000 after the Audi 5000 car, which got recalled and is a rare sight nowadays. "Yo, we outta here, 5000, G!" Ice Cube and Flavor Flav (I'm only out for one thang 1990]).
502	(n) 25 years ago, California had a vehicle code 502 for drunk driving. The current code is 23152(a) VC. Fuck the police and a 502 N.W.A. (8-ball [??]).
504	(n) New Orleans area code.

The word used	**It's meaning**
5150	(n) 5150 is the section of the California Welfare and Institutions Code dealing with involuntary confinement of a mentally disordered person. (I.e. California law consists of 29 codes, of which the Welfare and Institutions Code is one, and 5150 is a section number in that code.) Also the name of an old Van Halen album. It is also a track on Da Luniz album "Operation Stackola." 1)
64	(n) A 64-ounce bottle of malt liquor. "40's are no more because now I'm drinkin 64s" - Grand Puba (Three Men at Chung King) 2) (n) A 1964 Chevrolet Impala. "Jumped in the 64 with the diamond in the back, sunroof top." N.W.A. (Gangsta, gangsta [1988]).
Afro	1)(n) Hairstyle like the Jackson Five had, much hair and round like a ball. 2) (n) Person with an afro. *"Afro picks afro. chicks, I let my soul glow from my Afro dick"* Ludacris (Southern Hospitality (2000)
AK/AK-47	(n) Assault rifle of Russian origin, nowadays produced in China. The letters stand for "avtomat Kalashnikova" an automatic assault rifle invented by Mikhail Kalashnikov, who invented the gun in 1947. "My AK-47 is the tool" - Da Lench Mob (Freedom got an AK [1993]) (originally from NWA (Straight out of Compton)).
Al B Square Mall	(n) Albee Square Mall in Brooklyn - Bizmarkie

The word used	It's meaning
Aliz & eacute;	(n) French beverage made from passion fruit and cognac.
All that	(adj.) in possession of all the qualities.
Alpine	(n) Make of car stereo from a Germany-based company (http;// www.alpine.de). From the name of the manufacturers of the top in-car speaker systems. "Sit back and let the Alpine blast" - Jazzy Jeff & The Fresh Prince (Summertime [1991]).
Am	(n) The morning, as in A.M. "Steppin to the am" -- 3rd Bass (The cactus album [1989]).
Amarredos	(n) Italian bit-size cookies that often come with meals, "eatin better amarrettos." - 2 (n) From the neighborhood. "From around the way" Beastie Boys (No sleep till Brooklyn [1986]).
Axe	(v) Ask. "Gave her ten dollars, then she axed me for some more" - Schoolly D. (P.S.K. (what does it mean?) [??]).
Ay yo trip	(interj) Phrase to seek attention, compare "Check this out.".
b-boy	(n) From "break boy"; one who break-dances. B-boys in the front, back, side and middle, check out my b-boy rhyme and riddle- Schoolly D. (B-boy rhyme [??]).
B-Town	(n) Berkeley, California.

The word used	**It's meaning**
Bag up	1) (v) To laugh real hard at something. 2) (v) To be caught or arrested by the police. 3) (v) To have sexual intercourse with."Bag up bitches from John Jay." Nas (One L [1994]).
bail out	(v) Run away for someone
baller	1) (n) Ballplayer, someone who is good at playing basketball, and has moved up to earning a lot of money and getting a lot of girls from that. "I wish I was a little bit taller, I wish I was a bailer." Skee Low (I wish [??]). 2) (n) someone who has established himself in the hood, who is making much money (be it illegitimate or not), and who is good with the ladies; it is a Blood term. The Crip version of this word is "high roller."
ballin	(v) Having it all.
Bama	1) (n) Person who cannot dress well, a loser. Short for Alabama, meaning a person from the country, backwards unsophisticated. "Me and the rest of the bama's" Question Mark Asylum (Deriving from the D.C. area [??]). 2) (n) Shake, a type of marijuana from the leaves rather than the buds of the hemp plant.
Bang	(v) to fight, or to kill
banger	1) (n) someone associated with gangs and murder. 2) (n) Rocker, from head banging.

The word used	**It's meaning**
Bank	(n) Money. "That's cool cause I whipped out bank." Sir Mix-a-lot (I got game [??]).
Bankhead Hwy	(n) Highway in Atlanta where all the players go. Battle Bay Plaza
Battle	(v) To compete, usually freestyle rapping, sometimes break dancing or graffiti. "You want to rap and you got no battle, it's like havin a boat and you got no paddle." -Public Enemy (??? [1987]).
Bay Plaza	(n) Movie theatre in the Bronx - Nice and Smooth.
Be geese	(interj) To leave. "Yo we be geese" beam me up Scotty (interj) Give me crack cocaine.
Beamer	n) Expensive European car: BMW, status symbol. Used by Tribe Called Quest on Low End Theory. References to 325s are to BMW 3-series models with a 2.5 litre engine. References to 735, 740, 750's are to models in the 7-series range of BMW models. The 750'L is the flagship model made by BMW. A reference to the a seven series model is found in Ice Cube's "Ghetto Bird." 850s (mentioned in Wu-Tang's "Can It All Be...") is to the BMW 850i Coup & cute;.
Bean	(n) head or brain

The word used	It's meaning
Bed Stuy	(n) Bedford Stuyvesant section of Brooklyn. Also called The Stuy. Radio Raheem wears a Bed Stuy T-shirt in the movie "Do the right thing" by Spike Lee.
Beef	1)(n) an argument or discrepancy with another individual or group of individuals. The following citation is from the book Juba to Jive: the dictionary of African-American slang, by Clarence Major. Beef n. (1930s-1940s; 1960s-1970s) an "old" word dating back to general criminal use in the thirties. For young black in the sixties and later it meant roughly the same as it had earlier: a complaint or argument; a disagreement in progress. 2) (n) Sexual meat, like a penis. "No service of beef... meaning to have sex" Ò NWA (Parental Discretion Iz Advised [??])
being [down] with something	(v) Favoring something, thinking the same way. "Howie Tee, are you with me?" -- The Real Roxanne and Howie Tee ((Bang zoom) let's gogo).
Bend	(n) A prostitute. "She was more than just a bend. Grand Puba."
Bent	1) (v) Drunk. "It doesn't matter if I'm dead sober or I'm bent" Heltah Skeltah (Therapy [??]). 2) (v) Sad. "You got me bent like elbows, amongst other things" - Outkast (Aliens [???]).

The word used	**It's meaning**
Benz	1) (n) Expensive brand of European car: Mercedes Benz, status symbol. "I used to get no play, now she stays behind me, 'cause I said I had a Benz 190" - N.W.A. (I ain't the one 1988]). 2) (interj) Used to acknowledge "Audi", meaning goodbye.
Benzi-box	1) (n) A pull out radio. "Here come the cops... put the Benzi-box under the seat" Naughty by Nature (Strike a nerve [1991]). 2) (n) a box full of Mercedes Benz emblems that were stolen off the cars
berry	(n) a police car. The red lights on old cop cars looked like a berry on top of an ice cream. "Berry flashing those high beams" refers to a cop behind your car signaling for you to pull over. "Didn't even see a berry flashing those high beams" " Ice Cube (Today was a good day [1993]).
BG	1) (n) Baby gangster, as opposed to OG. An OG has shot some body, a BG has not shot any one yet. "I quit cuz of recess, you fuckin BG" -- Snoop Doggy Dogg (Pump [1993]). 2) (n) Black Gangster.
Bill	(n) A one hundred dollar banknote.
Bima	(n) See beamer. "Lex, coupe, bimaz, benz" -- Lost Boyz (??? [1996]).
Bird	(n) Kilo. "A bird in the hand" - Ice Cube (A bird in the hand [1991]).

143

The list goes on, and on and are just too many to list in this chapter. However, the author believes that there is enough information in this chapter to make the point about RAP music and that it is not just for dancing or singing. It is also used as an attempt to glamorize the gang culture.

CHAPTER 10

TEAM HATS AND WHAT THEY MAY SIGNIFY

Youngsters in school, who dress in clothing, or in this case, baseball hats may be showing an interest in gangs, or are already hard-core gang members. A perusal of the following list of team hats will show that just about every team hat can be used by a gang member to show allegiance to a gang, or as a "put down" of a rival gang. Therefore, everyone must be cautious about labeling kids as potential or hard-core gang members.

The author suggests that the readers look at other factors before labeling or singling out a student as gang member. These hats will, however, attract the attention of gang members. If the student is not a gang member and unknowingly wears one of these hats they could be putting themselves in extreme danger. Too many young people are getting shot at, or killed for wearing the wrong color clothing, red or blue, now the hats present an additional problem to teachers, administrators and parents. For the sake of every one in the school sites, the author recommends that it is very important that students not be allowed to wear any item that gang members use to identify a gang. This chapter will show how almost every sport's hat is used to identify gang membership, or to "put down" rival gangs. This will be a difficult task for schools and administrators to implement, but something needs to be done.

The following information details current ways in which gang members are using popular sports hats and clothing to represent individual gangs. Both professional and college teams are represented. It should be noted, again, that wearing sports clothing does not always signify gang affiliation. This list was compiled to make the reader aware of possible gang involvement. For further information "Log on" to: http://www.gangsorns.com/clothes 1 .html or http//www.tyc.state.tx.us/prevention/clothing.html. More information is contained in "The gang Resistance is Paramount (G.R.I.P) program in Paramount, California."

The main source is from Texas Youth Commission, Prevention Summary 3/23/02

TEAM	GANG	USEAGE
Atlanta Braves	People	Initial "A" for Almighty
Boston Celtics	Spanish Cobras	Colors: Green/Black
British Knights	Crips	Initials "B" & "K" for Blood Killers
Burger King	Crips	Initials "B" & "K" for Blood Killers
Charlotte Hornets	4 Corner Hustlers	Initials "C" & H
Charlotte Hornets	Imperial Gangsters	Colors: Black/Pink
Chicago Bulls	Vice Lords	Colors: Black/Red Latin Counts
Chicago Bulls	Black Peace Stone	"Bulls" stands for "Boy" You Look Like "stone Nation"
Chicago Black Hawks	Vice-Lords	Colors: Black/Red-Pitchfork Scar

TEAM	GANG	USEAGE
Chicago Cubs	Spanish Cobras	Initial "C"
Cincinnati Reds	4 Corner Hustlers	Put a "4" next to the "C" and an "H"
Colorado Rockies	Simon City Royals	They place a White "S" in front of the "C"
Columbia Knights	Bloods	Initials "C" & "K" for Crip Killer
Converse AII Star Shoe	People	Five point star in the logo of label
Dallas Cowboys	People	Five point star
Denver Broncos	Black Disciples	Switch "DB" for initials BD"
Detroit Lions	Gangster Disciples	Colors Black/Blue
Detroit Tigers	Folks	Initial "D" for Disciples
Detroit Tigers	Gangster Disciples	Colors: Black/Blue

TEAM	GANG	USEAGE
Duke	Folks	Colors: Black/Blue; "Duke" = Disciples Utilizing Knowledge Everyday
Duke	Folks	Crown going down means disrespect to Kings
Georgetown	Folks	Initial "G" for Gangster
Georgetown Hoyas	Gangster Disciples	Colors: Black/Blue; "Hoyas" stands for Hoovers on your ass
Georgia Tech	Folks	Initial "G" for gangster
Indiana University	Imperial Gangsters	Initials "I" & "U" Over lapping appear to make the shape of a pitchfork showing Folks affiliation
Kansas City	Royal/Folks	Colors: Black /Blue
Kansas City Royals	Simon City Royals	Royals
LA Dodgers	Gangster Disciples	Initial D for disciples
LA Kings	Latin Kings	Kings

TEAM	GANG	USEAGE
LA Kings	People	Kings stand for "kill Inglewood Nasty Gangsters"
LA Raiders	Folks	Raiders stand for Ruthless Ass Insane Disciples Running Shit
LA Raiders	People	Raiders stand for Raggedy Ass Iced Donuts Everywhere Running Scared Used To Disrespect Folks.
LA Raiders	Gangster Disciples	Colors
LA Raiders	Maniac Latin Disciples	Colors
Louis Vitton Cap	Vice-Lords	Initials LV reversed
Miami Hurricanes	People	Color: Orange
Miami Hurricanes	Future Stones	Color: Orange
Michigan	MLDS	Initial "M" for Maniac Latin Disciples
Minnesota Twins	MLDS	Initial "M" for Maniac Latin Disciples

TEAM	GANG	USEAGE
NY Yankees	Gangster Disciples	Gangster Disciples
NY Yankees	Norteño	Norteño Youth
North Carolina Tar Heels	Folks	Color: Black/Blue
Nike	Folks	Colors: Black/Blue
Oakland "A"	Ambrose	Initial "A" for Ambrose
Oakland A's	Orchestra Albany	Initials "A" & "O"
Oakland A's	Spanish Cobras	Color Green
Orlando Magic	Folks	"Magic" stands for Maniacs (MLDs) And gangster in Chicago. Colors: Black/Blue represents many "Folks"
Philadelphia Phillies	People	Initial "P" for people
Phoenix Suns	Black Peace Stone.	Colors: Initials "P" & "S" Nation

TEAM	GANG	USEAGE
Pittsburgh Pirates	People	Initial "P"; colors: Black/Gold for Latin Bloods Kings. And initial "P" for Pirius (bloods)
San Francisco	Folks	Switch initials for Giants Super Gangster Folk
San Francisco Giants	Future Stones	Initials S & F Spelled backwards
San Francisco Giants	Stone Freaks	Initials S & F
St Louis Cardinals	Spanish Vice Lords	Basic re-colored hat
Tampa Bay	Gangster	Disciples Color: Lighting Black/Blue
Texas Rangers	People	Initial T looks like pitchfork going Down
U of Illinois	Folks	Initials U & I together appear to be a pitchfork being thrown up Red/Black;
UNLV	Nation United	spelled backwards stands for Vice Lord Nation United

Hopefully this will be of some value to the readers of this book! Of course more team hats are used to send gang messages that are not included in this chapter because the author does not know more than those listed in the chapter, but hopefully, the reader can add more hats as they experience gang violence and participation in the schools. Moreover, as in all other things in this book, team hats can change meanings when the gang members realize that teachers, parents and other community members understand the original meaning.

CHAPTER 11

GANG GRAFFITI

Every town/city, urban or rural, will have it's own method of writing graffiti, but graffiti alone does not signify that it is related to a gang. There are many kids who paint graffiti on walls, but they are not gang members, they are known as "taggers." The taggers motives for painting graffiti could be, to show their artistic talents and are simply show off, they are simply defying law enforcement, or they like the challenge of doing it and getting away with their deed. Normally taggers leave some word or symbol to show their identity. Some of the graffiti is indeed very artistic. However, they cause a lot of damage to structures and bridges and should not be tolerated because it is destructive behavior.

This chapter is about gang graffiti and that is it's purpose. The author emphasizes again that not all graffiti is gang related. Gang members use graffiti to establish territories for selling drugs. They also protect their graffitti from rival gangs, and often use violence or death to protect their turf. Some of the gang graffiti has appeared at K-12 schools whereas the taggers usually do not use schools to "display" their art.. However, the key word is USUALLY. The author begins this chapter with the following guide to help the reader make some sense when viewing or reading graffiti.

Commonly Found Graffiti in the Los Angeles and other cities information taken from: Sawyer, David. A Parental Guide to understanding Gang influence" The Clovis Unified School District. Undated

C.R.I.P.S.	MOD	XIV
BLOODS	LB	OB
NORTE	BDG	F-14
ESF14	NIPS	X3
F-13	NVP	209
107	TRG	KMD

sur	sureños (southern) and use the roman numeral XIII
nor	norteños (northerners) and use the roman numeral IX

EXAMPLE FOR READING LATINO GANG GRAFFITI FOUND IN THE LOS ANGELES AREA

Steps for reading the graffiti, it is read like normal English, that is, from left to right and top to bottom, but that is about all references to English grammar. Following are some examples from the Los Angeles County: We can see it as:

B HG R
PQS
-13-
L/Ls

These are steps on how to read the above:

STEPS   GRAFFITI

Step 1:

B" means Barrio/varrio Meaning neighborhood   B
Group/clique

Step 2

The "HG" means Hawaiian Garden's
Gang or Clique (LA County)   HG

Step 3

The letter "R" is meant to be "Rifa" which means Rule,
reign, or Control.   R

Step 4

The actual gang group abbreviation of pequeños
from Hawaiian Gardens. It means younger
group, i.e. chicos midgets, tiny,
Or perhaps wanna bees

PQS

Step 5

The number 130 stands For "Sureños" meaning
Southern California. They are the Mexican Mafia
(M) is the 13th letter Of the alphabet)

13

Step 6

The letter "L" or "Ls" is used to mean vato locos or the crazy
ones/brave ones. Not normally a separate gang

L/Ls

Following are examples of the alphabet that can be written in various ways.
How each one is used depends on who is writing the graffiti. However, as can be
seen this type of writing can be very beautiful. We hope it will help the reader to
read graffiti. These pictures come from Merced California, a town of approximately
65,000 inhabitants.

GRAFFITI FOUND IN A SMALL TOWN NAMED MERCED

THIS IS WHERE THE GRAFFITI WAS FOUND AND PHOTOGRAPHED
IN MERCED CALIFORNIA: THE FOLLOWING THREE PAGES SHOW
THE GRAFFITI

LATINO GANG MEMBERS GRAFFITI

This is an anti Norteño graffiti. Note the # 14 on the neck of the picture and the right hand shows the number 4 with two fingers forming an X, which could mean "wipeout." The 4 Stands for 14 and 14 is the Norteño finger sign. In some cases it could also mean "West side" gang.

The last two letter are I3 (the second letter is not a "B" it is a 3 which stands for Sureños

This definitely a warning sign for Norteño gangs

Picture of shooting gun and the right hand displaying the number 4 (14) with a wipeout X, this means shoot the Norteños.

AFRICAN AMERICAN GANG GRAFFITI

This writing is difficult to read, but it can be read easily. If we read it carefully we can decipher it. It reads CRAZY YOUTH CRIP OUTLAWS (C. Y. C. O.) "DICIPLE."

Note: C.Y.C.O., same as last photo. However, this also includes the hand signal showing the number three; the sign for the CRIPs.

Most graffiti can be read if the reader uses their imagination. As can be seen from these examples, or photographs they depict violence of some kind, or against other gangs. On the other hand "tagging" by taggers normally does not depict violence. Moreover, a lot of graffiti is beautiful writing that denotes unbeautiful results.

CHAPTER 12

GANG TATTOOS

The slang words for tattoos may be Tats, Tacs, or Ink. This are the nick names of many tattoos, as used by gang members. Many of the tattoos that gang members use have been done while a gang member is incarcerated. However tattoos are now used on the bodies of various young people that have never been incarcerated. On the other hand, many tattoos on older people may be from their navy service, or who are veterans of all services.

However, tattoos have been popular for sailors for a very long time. Currently, many middle class youngsters and other young people also have had tattoos painted on their bodies. Consequently, it must be emphasized that not all tattoos are gang related. However, some high school students may have them on their body where they can be seen by their homies and only these will be addressed in this chapter for the benefit of parents, agencies and educators.

Tattoos on gang members are used for identification of the individual gang affiliation and they are often used to intimidate other students and to obtain new recruits. Keep it in mind that many gang members or wanna bees do not want to be identified and may not have them where they are visible to others. Moreover, the Asian gang members do not use tattoos for identification, nor to show off because they view tattoos as demeaning when placed on the human body.

SOME IDEAS FOR UNDERSTANDING TATTOOS.

1. If the tattooed picture is a gun, on a gang member, and it is pictured from the side; this means that person is carrying a gun.

2. If the tattooed picture is a gun, on a gang member, and it is pictured outward, it means that the person is a shooter, or a "hit man."

163

COMMON TATTOOS	THEIR MEANING
1. One laughing face and one crying	Play now, pay later, or my face happy life, my sad life.

COMMON TATTOOS	THEIR POSSIBLE MEANING
2. SWP	Supreme White power
3. Peckerwood	White pride (females)
4. Featherwood	White pride (females)
5. Viking themes	Common Caucasian tattoo
6. 100% pure	pure white or Anglo
7. SUR	Southerner (Sureños)
8. Norteños	Northerner (Norteños)
9. Mexican mafia (Sureños) hand with the letters Mexican mafia or eme	Eagle with snake in its mouth black sitting on the letters eme (In the palm Spanish it means the letter M). Also a black hand with the letters "eme"
11. Nuestra Familia/La familia Gang sombrero covering (Norteños)	"NF" NS, or a a machete dripping with blood.
12. Aryan brotherhood	Swastika covered with a 3-leaf clover. In the leaves of the clover are "AB" and 666

When viewing tattoos on K-12 schools they don't always mean gang affiliation.

Many young people shopping in malls often have tattoos, but they are not violent, nor gang affiliated. Therefore, the viewer should not stereotype youngsters with tattoos. On the other hand, if the tattoo projects violence of any kind, then the reader must be very cautious and perhaps report it to law enforcement agencies.

EPILOGUE

It is hoped that this book on gangs and school violence has met it's purpose, which is to alert society that these issues are present in all of society and will continue to increase unless society takes back the communities from the gangs. It is also hoped that with the information on school violence will help identify school shooters and prevent school shooting in the future. However, it must be noted that many of these problems still exist in the year 2005. The local newspaper, The Merced Sun Star had this to say,

> Being scared to go to school is just a day-to-day life for some kids. Some youngsters said, "I know you guys do your best to keep the schools safe, but the school didn't do its job. Another youngster opted to transfer to independent study when the youngster felt too unsafe to attend school. The school made me feel like they weren't caring about me. Said another. The Merced Sun Star May 2004. (It is unfortunate that these issues continue.)

Consequently, the information for teachers, parents, law enforcement, and the total community was meant to illustrate that prevention far out-weighs punishment. Prevention is a form to not only prevent, but also to deter, minimize, or even win the war against the destructive behavior of the youth. This book intended to provide information for the knowledge of gang membership and the inclusion of tattoos, RAP music, team hats and other issues will help to identify gang members, and school shooters to better address these violent acts.

This book does not pretend that it will completely stop gang and school violence. But is hoped that it does present a beginning toward the decrease such violence and to that end the author recommends that this book be a resource for the total community. The author also believes that this book is a start and will gladly accept any and all suggestion so that the book can be updated periodically. The author does not have all the answers, but does want to improve the situation of gangs and school violence.

An appropriate ending to this book is to quote the Modesto Bee, July 18, 2004 California and The Monterey County Post. July 22, 2004. Front page Modesto Bee, page B6.

The Stanislaus County Sheriff's Office has stated, or believes:

> There are three phases in dealing with gang violence, say experts, in the arena of Prevention, intervention and rehabilitation. 18 of the county's 30 murders this year are gang related. The Merced Sheriff's office believes the majority of is 8 murders are gang related "including one where a 13 year old pulled the trigger." A few innocents have gotten in the way of violence and have been killed"
>
> I think there are a large number of people in this county who are in denial. They think it is gang-banger killing other gang bangers, but we have had two women killed in the last six months who were not the intended targets. The Stanislaus County Sheriff stated, "We're not going to throw away 10,000 kids in this county. But on the other hand, we are going to jail anyone who is hurting others. We're not going to coddle them, we're not going to baby them. People who are out there doing drive-by shootings, killing people, maiming people-we're going after them. It's going to be heavy suppression.

The Modesto community is planning on preventing gang violence. They have suggested things that can be done such as: "National Night Out," Gang task forces, working with the Catholic church, meet with elected officials, obtaining and using money from grants, but they did not include the teachers and parents.

The Monterey County Post stated in the summer of 2004:

> "Unfortunately, for too long society has allowed the proliferation of these violent groups of youngsters because adults do not understand that the total society must work toward the same end. Society can no longer rely on schools and law enforcement agencies to address this problem. It is a societal problem and society is ultimately responsible for ending, or decreasing all violence in the schools and the communities.

As was stated, in so many words, throughout the book, **"if society is not part of the solution then it is definitely part of the problem!"**

BIBLIOGROPHY AND RESOURCES
FOR THE BOOK

REFERENCES FOR THE ARTICLES AND BOOK ABOUT GANGS AND SCHOOL VIOLENCE

PUBLISHED REFERENCES

Ban, J. R. (1993). Parents assuring student success (PASS): Achievement made easy by learning together. Bloomington, In.: National Education Service.

Bodine, R. J., & Crawford, D. K. (1998). The handbook of conflict resolution education: A guide to building quality programs in schools, San Francisco: Josey-Bass.

Borg, M. G. (1998). The emotional reactions of school bullies and their victims. Educational Psychology, 18, 433-444.

Brendtro, L., Brokenleg, M., & Van Bockern, S. (1990). Reclaiming youth at risk: Our hope for the future. Bloomington, In.: National Education Service.

Charney, R. S. (1998). Teaching Children to care: Management in the responsive classroom. Greenfield, MA: Northwest Foundation for Children.

Christenson, S. L. (1995). Families and schools: What is the role of the school psychologist? School Psychology Quarterly. 10(2), 118-132.

Craig, W. M., & Pepler, D. J. (1997). Observations of bullying and victimization in the schoolyard. Canadian Journal of school psychology, pages 13, 41-60.

Dr Dubar, Edward, Youth Violence: An Evolving Area for Psychological Intervention. CPA Briefings Number 154 December 2001.

Epstein, J. L. (1992). School and family partnerships: Leadership roles for school psychologists. In S L. Christenson & J. C. Conoley (Eds.
Home- school collaboration (pp. 215-243). Silver Spring, MD: The National Association of School Psychology.

Feedman, M. (1993). The kindness of strangers; Adult Mentors, urban youth, and the new Voluntarism. San Francisco: Jossey-Bass.

Journal "The American Psychologist" and in the Oct. 2001, Vol. 56 Number 10 pages 797 and 800.

Hayden, Tom a former California State Senator "No safe place" Source and date unknown.

Kauffman, James (1994). Violent Children and Youth: A call for action. Journal of Emotional and Behavior Problems, 3, pp. 25-27).

Lockyer, Bill (California Attorney General), Youth Violence: Clinical Theory, Research and Practice: Preventing Youth Violence. CPA Briefings Number 154 December 2001.

Lal (1991)

Lal et al., 1993, pp. 40-44-53. And pp. 33-43) 1993.

Morales, Gabe National Alliance of gang Investigators Associations, Latino Rap Chicano Music: An Influence on Gang Violence and Culture 3/23/02

Rainey, Maurice, Helping Youth Stay Out of Gangs, The Center for Human Services Training & Development. University Extension, University of California, Davis

Reece L. Peterson and Russell Skiba, Creating School Climates That Prevent school Violence. Date and source not listed.

The American Psychologist (APA Journal) The American Psychologist and in the Oct. 2001, Vol. 56 Number 10 pages 797 and 800.

"The Forensic Examiner" dated May/June 1999 and May/June 2000. The May/ June issue dealt with the article named, "Kids Who Kill" page 19.
Sawyer, David Gang Influence: a Parents guide to understanding gangs... Clovis Unified School District: Child Welfare and Attendance. Date not listed.

Psychologist Bryan Nichols, who works with the LA. Bridges gang diversion program,

David Oliver Relin "Teen People Nov. 2001, pages 126 & 27, July 2003

A Secret Service study in the fall of 2000

Texas Youth Commission, Prevention Summary 3/23/02

The Christian Science Monitor, Boston, July 15, 1996, front page and pages 10 & 11)

The Christian Science Monitor, Boston, 1996. "A boys one Day in a Gang."

Urban Education, Vol. 24 No. 3, Oct. 1989 pages 323-342. Sage Publications, Inc. 1989

Vigil, (1988) The article "Urban Education", Sage Publications, 1989

Walz, Garry, Gangs in Schools. Clearing House on Urban Education Digest. Eric Clearing House on Counseling and Student Services. Also in http://eric-web. tc.columbia.edu/digests/uds/dig 99gang.html 4/13/2002

UNPUBLISHED REFERENCES, HANDOUTS AT CONFERENCES, AND SOME NEWSPAPER ATICLES AND SAFEHOUSES

"A community Response to Street Gangs," prepared by the Kansas City, Missouri Police Department and Gang Squad

Mr. David Flores, Director, Alternative Education for the Los Angeles County Office of Education. Working With Gang-Involved Youth. A conference handout

Valdez, Al Street Gangs. Valdez Consultant Service 1997 (gang. 24hr. July 97)

Reference guide for help Crisis Resolution Center 1027 N. Van Ness, Fresno, Ca.

Comprehensive Youth Service 1617 E. Saginaw, Fresno, Ca. Clovis Youth Bureau 1033 5 St. Clovis, Ca.

"The Sanctuary" Fresno County EOC Youth Shelter
2336 Calaveras St. Fresno, Ca.

Sawyer, David. A Parental Guide to understanding Gang influence"
The Clovis Unified School District. Undated)

3. "Helping Youth Stay out of Gangs" The Center for Human Services Training
and Development University Extension, UCD Workshop materials for a workshop
conducted by Maurice Rainey, MA
A Children's Social worker with LA County.

Anchee Min, author of becoming Madame Mao, in an article titled "saves lives," in
USA Weekend page 4, August 6, 2000.

Merced Sun Star, Merced California 4/2/02 pages 1 & A6

Taken from Modesto Bee page B-7 April 2, 2001, Madison Shokley, and member of
the board of directors of the Southern Christian Leadership Conference-L. A.

Modesto Bee article dated 4/15/01 and authored by Connie Langland.

Modesto Bee article By Siobhan McDonough "Bullying can Foretell Troubled Later
in Life" dated Sept. 5, 2003.

(Taken from Modesto Bee page B-7 April 2, 2001, Madison Shokley, and member of
the board of directors of the Southern Christian Leadership Conference-L. A.)

(Paraphrased from People Magazine, June 4, 2001) In 1993... the Cherry Creek
School District in Englewood Colo. published Bully-proofing your school.

People Magazine, June 4, 2001)
Anchee Min, author of Becoming Madame Mao, in an article titled "Education
saves lives," in USA Weekend page 4, August 6, 2000

(Taken from Modesto Bee page B-7 April 2, 2001, Madison Shokley, and member
of the board of directors of the Southern Christian Leadership Conference-L. A.)

Modesto Bee Newspaper April 2, 2001. Modesto California.

The Cherry Creek School District in Englewood Colo. Published "Bully-proofing your school." And one of its co-authors is Dr. William Porter, a clinical psychologist.

RESOURCES REVIEWED AND SOME INFORMATION USED BUT NOT QUOTED DIRECTLY

Clearing House on Urban Education Digest 4/13/02

Valdez, Al National Alliance of Gang Investigators Associations Hispanic Gangs, a History of California Hispanic Gangs 1/30/02 (great resource on the history of Latino gangs)

INTERNET REFERENCES ABOUT GANG AND SCHOOL VIOLENCE

The Rap Dictionary to rec. music. hip-hop. It is extracted from the WWW version accessible at: http://www.rapdict.org/

http://eric-web.tc.columbia.edu/monographs/uds   107/gang_developing.html 3/24/2002

Developing a Gang Prevention Program. http://eric-web.tc.Columbia.edc/monographas/uds107/gangdeveloping.html

Morales, Gabe, (Gang Specialist, King County Correctional Facility) Chicano Music: An Influence on Gang Violence and Culture. National Alliance of Gang Investigations. http://www. Nagia. Org/Latino -rap.htm

Texas Youth Commission, "Gang Related Clothing." http://www. Tyc.state.tx.us/ prevention/clothing.htm

Our violet youth, Resource Manual, by Lewis & Associates, Provo Utah. 1998. Also @   HYPERLINK "http://www.qi3.com/end"   http://www.qi3.com/end gangs/home.html

Valdez, Al, (Investigator, Orange County District Attorney's Office) A History of California's Hispanic Gangs. National Alliance of Gang Investigations. http:// www. Nagia. Org/Hispanic-gangs.htm

Whitley, Ken Tattoos: Recognition and Interpretation. http://www. Convicts and cops. Com//tattoo.htm http://www.gangsoru. Com/clothes html. Gangs and Supporting Team Clothing

"http://www.gangsorns.com/clothes 1 .html"
http://www.gangsorns.com/clothes 1 .html

For more information, log on to HYPERLINK

Gabe Morales
http://www.ancieifire.com/biz4/sioovamowar
Last modified: January 30, 2002\ and http://www.nagia.org/latino_rap. htmponp

ISBN 141207733-8

44170140R00102

Made in the USA
San Bernardino, CA
09 January 2017